# LOOK AWAY!

# LOOK AWAY!

*Dixie Land Remembered*

Marion Cyrenus Blackman

*The McCall Publishing Company*

NEW YORK

*The McCall Publishing Company*
*230 Park Avenue*
*New York, New York 10017*

*Design by Tere LoPrete*

This book is for
The great-great-grandchildren
of
"The only private in the Confederate Army"

Look a - way!     Dix- ie Land.

*Dixie*, n., or *Dixie Land*. (Derived from *dix, dixie*, $10 note issued before Civil War by Citizens Bank of Louisiana, hence *land of dixies*, Dixie Land, in the South.)
—Webster's New International Dictionary

# I

---

When I look away! southward from Yankee Land now, it is
not to the land made overly familiar by song and story—the
black land of cotton plantations and pillared mansions, of
mighty, moss-draped oaks, of still-water bayous and cypress
knees, of magnolia and honeysuckle. No, the vista that comes
to my mind is vastly and bleakly different.

There can be few lands anywhere so ugly to look upon as
the cutover piney-woods hill country of north-central Louisiana where I grew up in the first two decades of the twentieth

century. The rapacious lumbermen ruthlessly swept the area bare of virgin pine timber with no selective cutting or reforestation programs and moved on, leaving ghost mill towns surrounded by stump-dotted acres of eroding reddish soil for miles around. The older agricultural communities, such as the one where my younger sister and I lived with our grandparents, were little affected by this invasion and despoiling, but their histories had never been bright nor hopeful. The redlands, with some sandy soil, were ill-suited to cotton, the one cash crop of the South then, and the people were as poor as their surroundings were cheerless.

These things I came to realize only later, for I was fourteen before I ever saw a city as large as Shreveport, and was several years older when I got my first glimpses of a mountain and the sea. I viewed my early scenes and circumstances with the unknowing wonder of youth, which fortunately clothes all vistas in a miraculous light.

Still, I think I must have sensed even then that something was lacking, at least in the landscape, for when I was quite small I went one day to a distant creek bottom in our Back Forty, dug up a pair of finger-size pin oak saplings and transplanted them to our sloping front lawn, one on each side of the path leading down to the high road. A few very old trees already shaded some neighboring houses, but my tiny ones were the first in front of ours. One survived.

When I recall my youth, I prefer to think of my pin oak tree rather than the cutover timberland, the unproductive soil, the unpainted gardenless habitations. It is certain that when I look away and back now there is some favorable distortion in my memories, making them pleasant on the whole, of growing up in an unlovely land.

My grandfather watched me transplant the pin oak saplings, using a posthole digger much taller than I to prepare holes for their tender roots. He offered no objection nor advice, but he did ask why I was doing it.

"Oh," I said vaguely, because I didn't really know why, "I thought we ought to have some shade for the house. It gets kinda hot after dinner on the front porch facing west." (Our noon meal was dinner.)

"Go to it," he said. "You may live to sit in their shade, but I doubt that I shall."

That discouraged me for a moment, because I had given no thought to how long it took a tree to grow to shade-size. It had not occurred to me either that there might come a time when Grandpa would not be there. But I went ahead with the project. Once they were upright in the ground, I noticed, they were just my height, about four feet, I would guess. For some reason that pleased me, and I fancied we might grow tall together.

The saplings survived the winter, as a few sparse leaves attested in the spring, but they did not seem to grow. They were still my height I observed as I examined them one day in May. Then I thought of something and hurried into the house to check. Sure enough, I had grown two inches taller since the previous summer. So had the saplings then, but that was not enough growth for a tree, as I realized even then. I cultivated them assiduously that summer, loosening the soil around them and applying fertilizer and water. The results were not noticeable.

I had my reward, though, the following summer when both of them shot up nearly two feet, with new limbs and leaves. They had left me far behind, but I didn't mind, for I had come to know by then that I did not have to grow as high as a tree to become mature and useful.

A few years passed—I can't recall just how many—and the pin oaks became sturdier and nearly ten feet tall. They began to look a little as real trees should, and I was proud. Then, suddenly, the one on the right side of the path began to show signs of sickness. The leaves wilted, then browned; and I noticed there were only shreds of bark on the trunk at the height of five or six feet.

I soon discovered the culprit: Old Black, our aged horse, who had the run of the lawn as well as the Near Pasture in back. He was using the pliant sapling to scratch the horsefly bites he couldn't reach with his teeth. Why he chose that one and never touched the other, I did not understand.

I built protective wooden pens around both, but too late to save Old Black's victim. It died, and I sorrowfully removed it. The one on the left side of the path continued to flourish. I was unable to find a suitable replacement of the proper size for the other one.

One year a pair of mocking birds came to nest in my pin oak. I was a proud host, not because I cared so much for birds, but because they had chosen as a home my property, now more than a bush, less than a tree.

I came home from school one day to find a neighboring farm boy shaking the still slender trunk, with the obvious intention of dislodging the nest. He was a head taller and twenty pounds heavier than I, but I snatched up a brickbat and rushed him with such fury that he took one startled look at me and fled. I think I would have tried to pound him insensible if I could have caught him.

I was afraid the shaking had broken or spoiled the eggs, but no, in due time they hatched. The fledglings thrived and eventually flew away. The parents came back the next year—or another pair came—and there was always a nest thereafter in the hospitable little pin oak.

The branches spread and thickened, and it became a truly

fine young tree, though yet far from grown. It cast a little patch of respectable shade in deep summer, not big enough of course to reach the front porch until too late in the afternoon to be appreciated, but adequate to provide a few square yards of real shelter from the midday sun.

I was pleased one hot Sunday to find Grandpa Blackman sitting in a chair under it, rereading *David Harum,* the only novel that ever appealed to him in his voracious search for book knowledge. It was a peaceful scene. A gentle breeze blew across the slope of the lawn, and the rustling canopy of the pinnatifid leaves offered the coolest spot on the premises, except for the fig tree in the back yard, which was in dank surroundings.

"You said you'd never live to sit in its shade," I reminded him. "You did, and you can many, many more times."

He nodded. "There's nothing finer than growing things, boy and tree alike," he said. "And when one is responsible for the other, it's wonderful."

Grandpa was feeling benign that afternoon, and the temptation is strong to portray him in what follows as being always in that mood. He wasn't, of course. Being only too human, he could be cranky, stubborn, and wrong-headed at times, as I now realize. In our occasional clashes, Grandma took my side as often as she sided with him but without appearing to do either. In retrospect, I can see that his strong prejudices against certain behavior patterns sometimes led him to condemn whole groups on the basis of his knowledge of perhaps only one individual member. He had a transcendent hatred of injustice, and when he was impulsively guilty of it even in a minor way, he always made amends. In nearly every concrete situation requiring him to act or pass judgment, his instincts served him and others well.

So I may be forgiven perhaps if I choose to be selective, overlooking his faults and remembering him at his best, as when he was relaxing in shade I was instrumental in providing and was philosophizing about the wonder of a boy and a tree.

One of the pleasant pastimes in the fall was hunting for and gathering wild fruits and nuts. The greedy lumber companies, although denuding the land of pine timber, had left untouched the copses of hardwood trees that grew along the banks of the creeks, some of them nut-bearing species. Rarest and most rewarding were the chinquapins, the dwarf chestnuts of the South. There was an occasional black walnut, and hickory nuts were plentiful. There also were persimmons, delicious after the first frost, inedible before. These trees near the banks of streams sometimes were hosts to muscadine vines. They twined among the branches and bore large, luscious grapes, growing singly, not in clusters. Commonest of all products of the wood were oak acorns, but these were of interest only to pigs and squirrels. When my pin oak was still little more than a sapling, I found an acorn under it one day. I recognized it at once as a white oak acorn, big as a thimble. . . . It had been put there by my sister Maude to tease me.

But there came a day when I found under it a true pin oak acorn. I peered into the thick branches and saw to my great satisfaction that they were loaded with many more. My tree had come of age, and I had hopes that it would live in the alien soil to attain the majestic size of full maturity.

The most miserable Fourth of July I can recall was spent on a cot under my tree. Working in a stave mill that summer, I carelessly got my foot under a log dolly, putting me out of action. Now, while others were enjoying picnics and fish fries, I was confined to a bunk of pain and a book under a modest shade tree on our front lawn.

As I lazed away the afternoon, I brooded a bit on the story Grandpa Blackman had told me recently about his second son, my father. He had been a doctor and a drinking man, an unlikely combination. Grandpa said sadly that he had been a brilliant weakling, unable or unwilling to face his responsibilities. He ran away from them one day and was never heard of or from afterward. That broke my mother's heart (or so my grandfather believed) and made her so uncaring about life that she died when my sister was born six months after he vanished.

On my cot, I worried a little over the fact that he and I shared the same blood and had been reared by the same good couple, whose blood we had inherited. I had not become familiar with the heredity versus environment debate, but I would not, could not, concede that because my father had turned out badly it was inevitable or even likely that I would do the same.

Thinking the long and confused thoughts of youth under my tree, I came to the solemn and unoriginal conclusion, which later proved comforting at times and frightening at others, that each person has his own special identity, a singular individual with a life of his own unlike any other, to be molded by a mind and will that are his alone, regardless of heritage or circumstances.

I left the grandparental roof soon after that for college and career. I returned to Grayson on two sad occasions a few months apart in the fall of 1924 and the spring of 1925 for the burials in Welcome Home Cemetery, first of Margaret Hodges Blackman, seventy-six, and then of Marion Clay Blackman, seventy-nine.

My pin oak had changed little in the few intervening years, and its future was still as uncertain in that barren land as was mine in a challenging career. . . . Many long years later, I had an impulse to go back and see how fared my tree half a century after it was planted. I did go back and I saw a fine specimen of *Quercus durandi*. But the real Dixie Land I revisited existed only down memory lane.

# II

Memory begins with a place-name: Manifest, which is near
Duty and Enterprise, not far from Utility, all in Catahoula
Parish in northeast Louisiana. Before that there was another
place-name, not remembered and seldom mentioned: Plain
Dealing, in Bossier Parish in northwest Louisiana. It was
there that my mother died after my father went away. My
grandfather journeyed two hundred miles from Manifest to
Plain Dealing and took back to my grandmother for rearing
an infant girl and an eighteen-month-old boy. They had al-

ready reared, educated, and seen married three sons and four daughters.

When we were approaching school age, my grandfather retired from farming, sold his cotton plantation in the Ouachita River bottom (which I do not remember), and moved to the village of Grayson in Caldwell Parish in north-central Louisiana, where a new consolidated school was being built. Founder and namer of the town was Wiley Branch Grayson, whose son Elias had married my Aunt Fanny Blackman. From him Grandpa Blackman bought a next-door, one-story, two-porch frame dwelling, with two cater-cornered forty-acre tracts of cultivated, grass-growing and timbered acres back of it.

My grandfather had no need whatever for more land than was required for a house site and vegetable garden, but he had been a grower all of his adult life and he still wanted to farm even if he had given up producing crops for sale. Ten acres would have been ample for a woodlot and a pasture for a horse and a couple of milk cows. But every year that he lived in Grayson, for as long as he was able, he planted at least twenty acres and sometimes more to corn, gathered it, and stored it in a crib for the winter. Another outbuilding was crammed with uncultivated and unbaled hay cut from the parcel of land just behind the house called the Near Pasture or from a meadow section of the Back Forty. A standing family joke involving Grandpa for a dozen years went like this:

"Why do you grow corn?"

"To feed my horse, of course."

"Why do you keep a horse?"

"To plow my corn, of course."

It was true that he felt a compulsion to grow at least one major crop, and in Grayson the obvious choice in that time of little diversification was corn, since it flourished reasonably well in the sandy loam of the so-called redlands, though never growing as high as an elephant's eye.

Grandpa had only scorn for the kind of cotton grown in that section of the state. He called it, not originally, "bumble-bee" cotton, because of the fanciful claim that such an insect could sit on the ground and suck nectar from the cotton blooms, so low were the stalks. Real long-staple cotton had grown man-tall on his black bottom-land plantation, and the yield was at least a bale to the acre, unfertilized. Only a measly third of a bale could be coaxed from the same unit of hill-country soil and that with the application of expensive commercial nitrate mixtures.

But he had other uses for a horse, or so he thought. An acre of land adjacent to the back yard was planted twice a year, spring and fall, to every kind of edible vegetable grown in that mild climate, and he preferred the horse-drawn field plows to prepare the soil rather than the hand-pushed tools favored by modern gardeners. Of course, a great deal of hoeing and raking was required in cultivating the garden produce after the plowing had been done, and I spent many backbreaking hours doing it, acquiring in the rebellious process my violent distaste for any form of manual labor, or even exercise.

A horse also came in handy for hauling bulky or heavy things, such as field crops, stove wood and winter firewood and kindling. But do you think Grandpa would buy a wagon, like everyone else with a need for transport? Not he.

Not being skilled with carpenter tools himself, he hired a man to build a contraption he called a "slide" for Old Black to pull. It was an eight-foot-long sled, nearly four feet wide, on wooden runners rising a foot above the ground. A bin about five feet deep could be placed on the platform to hold certain items such as corn, sweet potatoes, and pine knots, but most of the time he used the slide as a sort of low-level chariot. He either walked sedately alongside or behind it, or if in the mood, boarded it and rode in style and a certain impish pride to town and back for supplies that he couldn't grow —flour, rice, salt, sugar, and kindred staples.

It was the only such unwheeled vehicle in town—or the world for all I know to the contrary—and the villagers laughed at first, but soon came to accept it as just another of the eccentricities of Old Man Blackman. . . . I can hear now the exchange of bucolic repartee as he drove to the business section.

"Hop aboard, Henry, and take a joy ride with me."

"No, thanks. I'm particular who I ride with."

"Well, it's plain that I'm not, or I wouldn't have invited you."

Riding slowly on his slide—Old Black set his own pace— or walking along briskly at other times when he had no need for transportation or standing to talk for as long as anyone would listen, with one foot resting on a fence rail or a stump —in any posture he was a figure to command ready attention and to long remember.

He was of medium stature, of slight but wiry build, with small gnarled hands—and he looked like a veritable, disreputable tramp, a fugitive vagrant from some hobo jungle. He refused to have his hair cut except for special occasions; at such times he first shaved himself with a straight razor and then permitted Grandma to give him a crock clip with her sewing scissors. The rest of the time his beard grew untrimmed, and his flowing, untidy, gray locks straggled nearly to his collar under a battered and completely shapeless felt hat that he wore winter and summer. For the special events requiring his grudging decision to be shorn and shaven— usually funerals and meetings of the school board—he also donned his fading wedding finery. This consisted of a swallow-tailed coat, dark trousers of heavy cloth, and a remarkable hard-collar-flowing-cravat combination. A furled umbrella was optional.

In contrast, his everyday attire had to be seen to be believed. No poorest of sharecroppers would have worn his favorite garments to work, much less to mingle with fellow citizens in what passed for polite society. His shirts were coarse blue or hickory-colored cotton, collarless and faded. His pants were patched, baggy, and held up precariously with a length of rope tied around his waist. He didn't even own a leather belt, and his suspenders, called galluses, were saved for wear under the swallow-tail. He had two or three pairs of cracked, high-top shoes, but they had no laces, and how he kept them on his feet was something to wonder about. His always clean socks had holes in them, but he wore two pairs at once, each with unpatched gaps in the weave at different places, so that no hide ever showed through. In chilly weather, he protected himself with a wool sweater so old, so tattered, so shapeless and dispirited it must have been the first ever sold through the mails by Sears Roebuck. . . . No matter what he wore he was always immaculately clean in his person, thanks to a round zinc washtub and a kettle of hot water in the kitchen. Grandma kept his long johns and shirts as fresh as they were threadbare, with each washboard scrubbing threatening to be the last they could possibly survive.

The simple truth was that Grandpa just didn't give what he called a continental tinker's dam about his appearance and he couldn't believe that anyone else cared. Grandma did, but she eventually became almost but not quite resigned to his slovenly habiliments.

"My aim is to stay clean and covered, that's all," he would say on the increasingly rare occasions when Mother (his name for her) was moved to remonstrate with him. "Who looks at an old man, anyway, except in the face?"

A look in his face could be rewarding, because it was as mobile as a professional mime's and he was really rather handsome in an earthy patrician sort of way under his untended facade. But, more likely to be remembered than his profile or full-face features were the expressions that played over them, especially when he signaled emotions with his eyes. In the course of a five-minute conversation, they could run a gamut from wonder, to surprise, to amusement, to sorrow, to absolutely empty repose. One moment his serene blue eyes would twinkle with secret laughter and the next would mist over with sadness or compassion.

He loved to hear himself talk and rather fancied his own eloquence and expositive logic, but he could listen to others with sincere interest and sympathetic understanding of half-said things (a rare quality); and various persons, young and old, sought him out regularly to tell their woes, ask his advice, or just exchange views upon any subject they cared to mention.

Grandpa Blackman was not compelled by financial circumstances to look like a nomadic beggar fleeing from a village constable, and my grandmother certainly was not his feminine counterpart. She was rather plump, with a round face that usually reflected a mixture of placidity and undefinable sadness. Her hair was always neatly coiffed, and she appeared respectable at all times, whether in her Sunday best or in her everyday house dresses. True, like most women, she sometimes sighed in vain for household or personal fripperies that Grandpa regarded as unessential at best or nonsensical at worst. (These unsatisfied minor longings probably were not the reason for the remote sadness.)

Most of the townspeople thought my grandfather was rich.

He was not, but he was not a pauper, either. His financial status lay somewhere between. I never heard him or any member of the family say how much money he had saved during a lifetime of cotton farming and rearing and educating a large family, nor how much he was paid for his plantation when he retired. I never even learned where he kept his capital, in a Jena bank or a hollow tree, but the former seemed more likely. I do know he was able to pay outright the full price Grandpa Grayson asked for our eighty-acre farm and house.

Then, a few years later, when the forty-acre farm adjoining ours on the north, known as the "old Thompson place," was put up for sale, Grandpa promptly bought it for the asking price, with no mortgage; he was dubious about the kind of neighbor we might get if he didn't buy it himself. It had an older, larger and amply tree-shaded house on it, and Grandpa rented it and the land to others for years after buying it, picking his tenants carefully. On two occasions, when a prospective renter indicated a preference for a smaller house such as our first one, he simply moved us over to the Thompson place and let the tenant have ours as a domicile to go with the adjacent cultivated field. He didn't think either time to tell my sister and me that we were moving, and it was something of a shock to come home from school and find our home bare and all our belongings installed in the house next-door. But it was sort of fun, too, especially since neither of the two interludes of a home away from home lasted longer than one crop year.

The belief that Grandpa Blackman was wealthy undoubtedly grew out of the fact that Grayson had no bank when we first moved there, and he promptly filled the money-lending void. His banking practices were as curious as his personal appearances and habits, if less deceptive.

He would lend a hundred or a thousand dollars to anyone he trusted—and his judgment was uncannily good—with no collateral, just a demand promissory note. He never, to my knowledge, demanded repayment of principal as long as the interest was paid promptly until near the end of his life when capital funds ran low. But his peculiarity as a private banker was his insistence upon getting his interest payments each month, instead of annually, at the rate of five percent a year. He also lent money to his sons and sons-in-law on the same basis, discouraging repayment of principal, and a couple of them, both well off, still owed some monthly interest money to him when he died, and made payment to the estate.

He wished to collect what, because it dominated our lives, I came to think of in capital letters as INTEREST by the month, because that was the way he paid his bills. There were at one time seven general stores in a town that, even with its surrounding agricultural community, could barely support three or four profitably. We had charge accounts at all of them. Grandma and, in time, my sister and I could buy anything we needed within reason at any of them on credit, but the strictest rule in our household was that each purchase had to be reported immediately to him.

As is the custom everywhere, I eventually learned, the merchants kept books and collected once a month from their customers—if they could. The difference in my grandfather's case was that he meticulously kept his own ledgers, with entries of money lent, amounts of interest due and collected, and items charged to our accounts at the stores. (I have some of those fascinating old ledgers.) The sums he owed to the merchants each month were almost always greater by his figuring than by theirs, because he never forgot to jot down a pound of nails, or a box of salt, or a pair of stockings, and they sometimes did. (The worst tongue-lashing I ever received from Grandpa Blackman was when I forgot once to report charging a five-cent pencil and, for once, the merchant didn't forget.) In time the storekeepers gave up entirely keeping track of purchases in the name of M. C. Blackman. They simply took the sums he gave them at the end of each month and entered them under "Accounts Paid."

Somehow, the charge accounts at the stores always seemed to balance the total each month, almost to the penny, of the INTEREST Grandpa collected from his debtors. There was never any cash left over, and no merchant ever had to wait another month to be paid. More than once I heard it said of someone that he was "honest as Old Man Blackman," and it gave me a warm feeling.

Grandpa never had nor wanted a cent of money on him. Until I was old enough to be paid for chopping and picking cotton on other farms or for working in a sawmill or stave mill, almost the only money I ever had was in nickels and dimes Grandma gave me from her private teacup hoard on a kitchen shelf. She deposited in this bank some of the money she received from the sale of surplus eggs and butter against the time when she would want to send a money order for catalogue articles from the mail-order houses not available in the local stores.

Six of the stores sat in a bleak row along the wide, unpaved main thoroughfare on the west side of the railroad. (The seventh was on the high road on our side of the tracks.) All except one in the row had fake fronts, which deceived no one into believing they were two-story structures. The forthright exception was a long and narrow one-story frame building with a gable roof, which squatted against the gentle back slope like a dog on its haunches. Grandpa was impartial in our credit patronage of the merchants, but once when I was about ten he suggested it would be a kindness to make purchases when possible at this particular store, operated by a kindly, stooped old man named C. C. Roark (the initials stood for Christopher Columbus, but nobody ever called him Chris, or anything but Mr. Roark). Grandpa did not explain his unusual request, but I learned the reason myself before very long.

There were two things about the Roarks that struck me as peculiar. One was that they had been married for many years and had no children. At that time, I did not realize it was possible to be old and married and childless. Later on, my grandfather told me that some married couples did not want children or were physically incapable of producing them, but there were no other examples in Grayson to my knowledge. At the time I heard, without understanding, the older boys of the town lewdly speculating on the reason for the childlessness of the Roarks.

The other odd thing about Mr. and Mrs. Roark was that they lived in the rear part of the store. All the other merchants and their families lived in houses well apart from their places of business.

Actually, the Roark living quarters were quite separate from the store, except that the same roof covered both. There was not even a connecting door. Each weekday morning, rain or shine, Mr. Roark emerged from his home at the rear and walked around to the front of the store, climbed a steep flight of stairs to a high porch, and unlocked the double doors with a large, fat key.

Near the back end of the long building, and at its side, overlooking a dirt road leading west from the "main" street, there was a narrow porch recessed under the eaves. That was the entrance to the "house."

Inside, it was like any other one-story dwelling, with a living room, bedroom, dining room, and kitchen, and it was hard to remember that just beyond a wall was a general store. One reached the porch through a picket gate and a yard full of flowers. The porch itself and a swing that was its only furnishing were almost entirely obscured in summer by a screen of broad-leaved vines.

One of my chores was to deliver twice a week to Mrs. Roark for resale to the customers of the store or for her own use a pound of butter and a dozen eggs from my grandmother's surplus. In the hot months, I timed my delivery to coincide with Mrs. Roark's afternoon nap, so that I would have an excuse to sit for a while on the cool, quiet porch, where slanting yellow sunlight on the flowers could be seen through a pattern of green leaves, producing a soothing effect.

After her nap, Mrs. Roark usually found me daydreaming there and exclaimed, "Why, Marion, you naughty child, you've let my butter get all runny." I did not take her scolding to heart, because she was often referred to as "a grandmotherly soul," a description meaning that she was kindly. I thought it an odd term considering that she had never even been a mother, let alone a grandmother.

She usually asked me in for refreshments, which most often were teacakes. Occasionally, there would be a bottle of pop from the store to wash them down, and I liked that, because it cost a nickel and I seldom had one to spare for soft drinks. After my repast I would go around to the store with Grandma's very short list of items to take home in exchange for the eggs and butter. In keeping with Grandpa's suggestion, I would try to charge other things not covered by the payment for the produce if anything in the Roark stock was needed at home. I found myself of two minds about this, because at other stores to which I delivered dairy products there often would be a cash balance over and above the cost of items on Grandma's list, and I would be permitted to keep a coin or two for running the errand. But this never happened at Roark's; the old man had no cash to spare, as I learned.

At the front of the store, opening onto the high porch, at the left of the entrance, there was a window on which was painted:

C. C.  ROARK

DRY  GOODS

with the strip of wood that held the windowpanes in place running down the middle and separating the words into two groups. To the right of the entrance, on a similar window, was the lettering:

C. C.  ROARK

NO  TIONS

That second window puzzled me for a long time. I didn't know what TIONS were, and, whatever they might be, I couldn't understand why Mr. Roark felt obliged to advertise that he had none. I was ashamed to ask anyone, because nobody else remarked upon the curious sign, and I didn't want to appear ignorant. I looked up the word in a dictionary, but all I found was "–tion," a suffix pronounced "(shun)," and I wasn't sure I knew the meaning of a suffix. And though I examined the sign anew each time I went to the store, it remained the profoundest of mysteries.

One day, when I had no delivery to Roark's, Grandma asked me to get her a spool of Number Sixty black cotton thread from another store she knew carried it in stock. I decided to try Roark's first, but he shook his head and said, "Sorry, sonny, I'm all out of Number Sixty. Do you suppose your grandmother could make do with the Fifty?"

I said I didn't know. The fact was that I didn't know the difference between the Fifty and the Sixty, but I wasn't letting on that I didn't.

"Well, take her the Fifty," he said, "and if she can't use it, you can bring it back." He put the spool in a paper bag and perhaps by way of apology or prepayment for the extra trip I might have to make, handed me a stick of peppermint candy from a glass jar.

As he gave me the treat, he looked forlornly around the store. I did too and for the first time I became aware that its shelves and counters were more than half empty. He seemed so sad and resigned that at last I found courage to ask the question that had long bothered me.

"Mr. Roark, why do you have a sign saying you have no TIONS?"

He looked at me vaguely. "What did you say?"

I pointed to the window. "It says NO TIONS. Right there under your name."

He stared at the sign. From inside the store the second line read:

SNOIT ON

and I examined it backward and forward. Suddenly, I saw in my mind's eye the dictionary line "-tion," with the pronunciation in parenthesis, "(shun)," and I understood. I felt so foolish that I wanted to run out of the store, but Mr. Roark's continued puzzlement gave me a chance to recover. I managed to laugh.

"I was just joking, Mr. Roark," I said. "The way that word is separated, when I was little I used to think it said NO TIONS, and I wondered why you had a sign saying you had none. Of course I know what notions are."

Mr. Roark smiled and kindly fell in with the suggestion that my age of ten or so was pretty advanced. "I can see how a little fellow might have got mixed up," he said, nodding. He became sad again. "I guess I ought to fix that sign to read NO NOTIONS. I haven't had any notions in stock for a long time—or much of anything else. In fact, it might be more accurate to fix the other sign to say NO DRY GOODS."

He wasn't serious, of course, about doing anything to change the signs and he did nothing to fill his shelves, either. As I have said, the town couldn't support all of its stores profitably, and the childless Mr. Roark was old and had scarcely any incentive to continue the competition. The dwindling of his stock was timed nicely, however. Not very long after our conversation, Mr. and Mrs. Roark both died, within a couple of weeks of each other. The store shelves at the last contained only a few sacks of flour and two or three bolts of calico. I don't know what became of them, and the store-and-house remained unoccupied the rest of my time in Grayson.

Grandpa Blackman had done his compassionate best to stave off an unimportant little business failure, but his support was too little and too late. However, as I have noted, it mattered little to anyone, for there was none to mourn the Roarks and their empty store and lives—no one, that is, except Grandpa Blackman. He was choosy about the funerals he attended, but he put on his faded finery twice in one month and walked out to Welcome Home Cemetery, joining physically but ignoring in spirit the morbid little group that showed up for every burial there, no matter whose. Later, commenting on the services, he told me with the special preoccupied solemnity that always gave me the impression that he was not saying all he was thinking:

"I always feel that someone should shed an honest tear of regret for those who live and die, leaving behind them no mark at all that they ever existed."

For some reason, I felt like telling him about NO TIONS. He did not laugh.

"Words are like nearly everything else," he commented. "Sometimes you have to study them from all angles before you understand them thoroughly."

# III

---

The first general store in the north-south row along the main thoroughfare was a bit apart from the rest, across the west-bound dirt road from Roark's. It was the most prosperous of them all, and its owner was reputed to be the richest person in town, with far more validity than the speculation concerning the wealth of my grandfather. He was Albert A. Mixon, a lean, gray-complexioned man of indeterminate age. He gave year-long credit to dozens of sharecroppers on the extensive farmlands he owned, taking most of the bales of cotton they grew in settlement of the accounts; and he bought and sold cotton grown on other farms. Each fall, the vacant lot just north of his store was piled high with bales of cotton, all of which he personally stenciled in tar with the label "A. A. Mixon, Grayson, La.," before shipping them north.

He was the only real live Republican I ever knew until I was grown, and because of his politics and profession, he had been postmaster of Grayson since 1897, when the Republicans regained power with McKinley.

The post office, which, along with a storeroom, occupied the rear part of his store, consisted of a panel of rented lock boxes and a general delivery window, with office space behind.

Mr. Mixon had one store clerk, a short, stocky Dutchman named Theodore Seiler. Mr. Seiler had no official connection with the post office, but part of his job was to operate it, and he was the only one familiar with the full details. Mr. Mixon concerned himself only with signing the routine reports, which Mr. Seiler prepared.

Mr. Seiler was the father of Reginald, a good friend of mine though a year older, and of Elsie, who was my school classmate, and I knew from them that he liked the postal part of his work. The duties were not onerous. Four mail-and-passenger trains stopped each day in Grayson, one each way about two hours apart in the morning and one each way about an hour apart in the "evening," which in Grayson meant the period from midday to what was called "first-dark." After each train arrived, a boy who did odd jobs for Mr. Mixon carted the mailbags to the store. Mr. Seiler opened them, sorted the letters, junk mail, and packages, called "All up!" from behind the partition and stood by for a time at the general delivery window.

During the middle of the day, there would be only an

occasional request for stamps or a money order to interrupt Mr. Seiler's major occupation of measuring cloth, weighing lard, selling some NO TIONS, and bringing out sacks of meal and flour from the storeroom adjoining the post office. In busy periods, Mr. Mixon also waited on trade, but he was kept occupied for the most part in his private office, going over his accounts and dealing with his tenants, other cotton growers, and traveling salesmen, then called drummers.

If Mr. Seiler made no bones about liking the interludes behind the post office partition, he also did not conceal his distaste for his other duties, but he performed them with stolid proficiency.

Albert A. Mixon, postmaster, had been a fixture in our town for so long that it was almost inconceivable that anyone else would, or could, aspire to the office. . . . Then came the Presidential election of 1912.

It was the first one to which I had paid any attention, since it was held a few weeks after my tenth birthday and had repercussions down in Grayson that certainly never were known to or dreamed of by that oft-defeated Democratic candidate, William Jennings Bryan, when he used his still great influence to bring about the nomination of Woodrow Wilson instead of Champ Clark.

Grandpa had been about equally concerned and amused in following national politics since he reached voting age, to hear him talk on the subject, and in my time he was fascinated by the famous fundamentalist who was a recognized leader of the Democratic Party for thirty years. Grandfather neither knew nor cared much about bimetallism, but he often lovingly quoted the celebrated passage in the speech with which Bryan captured control of the convention in 1896 and won his first nomination for the Presidency:

"You shall not press down upon the brow of labor a crown

of thorns; you shall not crucify mankind upon a cross of gold."

Grandpa knew the entire speech, but it was the imagery and rotund phrases rather than the meaning of the Cross of Gold platform plank address that intrigued him. In fact, a story he was fond of repeating was one in which Champ Clark was reputed to have said to the governor of Illinois:

"You know, I've been rereading Bryan's speech. What did he say?"

After Wilson won by virtue of the vote splitting by his opponents, Theodore Roosevelt and William H. Taft, Grandpa remarked to a neighbor:

"I suppose the Great Commoner will be rewarded with the appointment as postmaster general, and one of the things he's certain to do through the party's patronage system will be to take away Albert Mixon's stamps and letters sideline."

Grandpa did not read newspapers, but he kept up with national affairs, in a manner of speaking, by subscribing cheaply to Brann's *Iconoclast* and a monthly farm magazine.

As it turned out, Bryan was appointed secretary of state, but in due time, after the inauguration in 1913, Mr. Seiler received through channels from the office of Postmaster General Albert S. Burleson a notice of a competitive examination to be held for the postmastership of Grayson, La., fourth class. As required by law, he posted it on the bulletin board near the lock box panel along with the "Fugitive Wanted" posters.

Although requirements for postal service employees had become stricter since his first appointment by McKinley, Mr. Mixon had no doubt that with proper coaching by Mr. Seiler he could pass the examination and qualify for the appointment—if taking the test really mattered. Being politically astute, he knew it didn't, so he made no application and resigned himself to being replaced by William (Uncle Billy) Broadway, or another of the staunchly Democratic merchants in the town.

It never occurred to him that his lowly Democratic clerk might covet the position, and that Mr. Seiler, besides being the only experienced potential candidate in Grayson, had over the years quietly made many friends among the local Democratic politicians by his courteous and efficient handling of the post office.

Mr. Mixon did not suspect what Mr. Seiler was up to when he asked for, and was given, a day off to go to the city of Monroe, thirty miles away. It was the day and place for the postmaster examination.

Hence, it came as a shock to Mr. Mixon when, not long afterward, Mr. Seiler silently laid before him the formal notification that he, Seiler, had been appointed postmaster of Grayson. Mr. Mixon was outraged at this perfidy and fired his long-time clerk before Mr. Seiler could resign, as he had intended to do all along if successful; although if he had wanted to and Mr. Mixon had been willing, there was no real reason why he could not have continued to do both jobs in the Mixon store. The only difference would have been that he would then be the official, rather than the unofficial, postmaster and would receive the emoluments of the position.

Mr. Seiler no doubt was sorry that Mr. Mixon was so upset, but he was too happy over his newly acquired independence to brood about it. He rented quarters down the street in a frame building erected for that purpose between the barbershop and A. C. Cloyd's store. He moved the government-owned post office equipment there, and genially took up the duties of postmaster, a position of considerable prestige in any small town. Under the shed overhanging the unpaved sidewalk, he installed a long bench, and it became the favorite hangout of elderly whittlers, young hellions, and other idlers. No women, of course.

Mr. Seiler's annual income, though small, probably equaled and may have exceeded his previous salary as Mr. Mixon's clerk and unofficial assistant postmaster, and he was rid of the dreary, daylong duties of a general-store clerk. He had plenty of middle-of-the-day opportunities for reading, napping, and working out chess problems. Mr. Seiler was a contented man.

Mr. Mixon was not. He could not have missed greatly what had been to him the comparatively small revenue from the postmastership, but he came to realize that, aside from giving him prestige, the post office had brought a great deal of trade to his store. Now, many customers who had come to Mixon's primarily for mail and money orders were shopping elsewhere, as were those also who had shopped at Mixon's because they liked Mr. Seiler. Mr. Mixon just couldn't forgive his ungrateful former employee, who not only had presumptuously succeeded him as postmaster but had used his job as Mr. Mixon's store clerk to obtain the office.

He not only did not speak to Mr. Seiler when they met on the street but he took the only retaliatory measure open to him. In those days, the income of the postmaster was determined largely by the volume of stamps canceled at his post office. For each cancellation he received a percentage, and the total became the basis for computing his remuneration. To this income Mr. Mixon refused to contribute.

First, by way of snubbing Mr. Seiler, he got one drummer after another to buy stamps for him at post offices in other towns, although stamp sales did not figure in the postmaster's income, and then he regularly posted all of his outgoing mail on the trains that stopped at Grayson instead of dropping it in a slot at the post office.

The latter procedure entailed a great deal of physical effort and some precise timing by Mr. Mixon. Twice each morning and evening, he had to listen from the front part of his store for the warning whistle of the incoming trains, which were seldom on time. Hearing the signal, he would set out, with his long-legged stride, for the depot platform, three hundred yards away. He would arrive, puffing, just in time to lay his half dozen or so letters on the floor inside the open door of the railway-mail car. These letters then would carry the railway-mail cancellation rather than that of the Grayson post office. Mr. Seiler's commissions thus were reduced by a trifling sum each month.

The spectacle of Grayson's richest citizen stalking to the depot two to four times a day with a handful of letters was at first puzzling to his fellow townspeople. Then, as the motive became generally known, his behavior was regarded as rather childish, if not ludicrous. Mr. Seiler continued to handle with scrupulous care Mr. Mixon's incoming mail, and said nothing publicly.

Grandpa was both amused and contemptuous. "That's the silliest bit of nose slicing to spite a face I ever saw," he told me and others. "The shoe leather he wears out costs more than the stamps he uses. But maybe the exercise will do him good and sweeten the vinegar in his veins."

Mr. Mixon must have become increasingly aware that his daily mail sorties were the subject of amused and, here and there, disdainful comment by many residents, but he stubbornly persisted in his retaliatory tactics throughout the first Wilson administration.

It would be more dramatic if I could report here that Mr. Mixon once missed a train and an important business deal as a result or that Mr. Seiler saved him in some manner from such misfortune, but nothing of the sort happened, as far as I know. The prosaic fact is that Mr. Mixon's unhappy status was prolonged beyond endurance by President Wilson's re-election in 1916, a calamity he had not believed possible. He began to retreat then, apparently deciding he couldn't face another four years in an attitude that even he now recognized as being more than a little ridiculous.

He began relenting by using envelopes with no return address and at night furtively dropping the letters into the mail slot in the front door of the post office, but of course Mr. Seiler quickly caught on to that, since he knew from long experience all of Mr. Mixon's business connections.

It was after Mr. Seiler quietly returned to him a letter with the notation that it had been addressed incorrectly that Mr. Mixon surrendered completely. Thereafter, he posted his mail openly in the post office and even nodded coldly to Mr. Seiler when buying stamps.

The ups and downs of politics ensured that things would not continue indefinitely as they were. I was working temporarily in a bank in Shreveport when the Republicans triumphed in the national elections of 1920, thus reversing the political potentialities of the postmastership in Grayson, as in thousands of other towns. In the winter of 1921, Grandpa wrote one of his rare and abbreviated letters, bringing me up to date on the postal service he was making use of to inform me:

A. Mixon has post office again. Has new clerk, too, or rather old clerk in new status, T. Seiler. Understand he made deal so no upsets if Democrats ever take over again. No matter who wins or who holds title officially, T. Seiler will be real postmaster at salary bigger than he got on his own for eight years. Or at Mixon's before that.

Everybody happy, townsfolks as much as anybody. A.

Mixon busy with accounts, and business booming again. Merchandise clerking done by two new salesladies; what world coming to, women working in public? Well, they got and deserved the vote, might as well get the jobs including public office. Can't do worse than men.

Nice new condition for T. Seiler, sells no goods, just sits contentedly at his desk behind lock box partition tending postal business and saying howdy to many friends. They come for mail, stamps, money orders and talk, but stay to buy. Like old times. T. Seiler even has time off afternoons to work out chess problems and dream a little while waiting for that evening mail. Still running late. So am I.

The unprecedented FDR Presidential era began in 1933, but the Mixon-Seiler entente presumably continued in effect, and the postal patrons of Grayson couldn't have noticed that Theodore Seiler again held the title of postmaster. His cheerful cry of "All up!" surely must have sounded the same under any administration.

# IV

The passenger-mail train that was late most often and longest was the southbound in the "evening." Perhaps it only seemed that way, because the four of us in the Blackman household usually sat together at that time of day as a family and observed its decelerating passage on the tracks a hundred yards beyond the lawn, downgrade toward the station for a reluctant pause of two or three minutes. This was the only hour in the twenty-four except at mealtimes when we were a unit, with the leisure to pay attention to a train and other matters of common interest. When the northbound arrived and departed an hour or so later some of us were asleep. The schedules of the morning trains, one in each direction with the same time separation pattern, found us scattered to our individual routines or special preoccupations.

I don't recall the exact time the southbound was due, but it was after early supper and preceded the sunset—by how much depended upon the season, of course. It was a lazy, almost somnolent interlude, relaxing and comfortable, pleasant to remember.

In balmy weather my sister and I sat on the edge of the front porch (called a gallery), our feet resting on the topmost of half a dozen wide, wooden steps. Our grandparents sat in rocking chairs behind a loosely constructed lattice supporting an American Beauty rose vine. This had climbed to spread and spread along the eaves to the juncture of the front porch with the side porch leading to the back yard.

This sort of scene required mood music, and Grandpa provided it. Among his other talents was the ability to play a fiddle by ear; he could not read music, but, unlike me, he was not a musical ignoramus and could pick up every note of a tune after hearing it once.

Sitting in his rocking chair after supper, Grandpa began by patting his right foot in the approved country fiddler style and sawed away at such familiar tunes as "Turkey in the Straw" and "The Arkansas Traveler." These were lively— too lively, in fact, to seem suitable to the peaceful occasion, so he would sit dreamily for a few moments and then begin to play softly something that was unrecognizable.

"What's that?" I demanded once. "I never heard that tune before."

"Not a tune," he said. "Has no name. I was just thinking on the fiddle. Sort of saying with music how I feel. You know:

nice evening after a good day's work . . . satisfying supper, and Mother not too tired . . . you children behaving yourself . . . glorious sunset . . . no worries now, and the immediate future looks rosy. . . . That sort of thing."

Grandfather either had never encountered "improvisation" as a musical term, or he thought it was a bit too much for my vocabulary at the time. I'm still a musical ignoramus, but my vocabulary has increased somewhat.

When the day waned, Grandpa would lower his fiddle to his lap, peer through the rose vine screen at the cloud reflections of the sun descending behind a house-and-treetop horizon, and remark, "Southbound's late again."

He had no watch, and the only clock in the house was a tall ornate one that sat on a bedroom mantelpiece and struck the hours if Grandma had remembered to wind it with a brass key that was kept inside under the pendulum. But he knew, anyway, when the southbound was due and behind schedule.

The whistle signal for the crossing would sound uptrack fifteen or twenty minutes later, and after the coal-burning locomotive had rushed past with its half-dozen cars rocking alarmingly behind it, Grandpa would stand up to go inside and get ready for bed by first-dark.

"Night is for sleeping," he said a thousand times. "Day for stirring around. Perhaps I should be more accurate and say night is for staying in bed and day for staying out it, health permitting."

My built-in chronometer was not as accurate as Grandpa's when I was small, and I became obsessed with the desire to own a watch for precise time telling. A watch at that time and place meant a Dollar Ingersoll, which ranked with a Model-T Ford for relative low cost, dependability and durability.

In my financial condition, however, a Dollar Ingersoll

seemed almost as unattainable as a four-hundred-dollar Ford. Nevertheless, so determined was I to own one that I dedicated the summer vacation from school before my eleventh birthday to accumulating the sum of one dollar.

Not to be too suspenseful, I succeeded, but I am sure I never would have made it except for what I came to think of as the "Half Dollar Miracle" at the old Thompson place.

It occurred during the first of the two separate years that we moved over there to our Second House to make way for a tenant who coveted our First House.

The money-earning opportunities open to an under-teenage boy in that place and time were limited indeed. I spent one wickedly hot day in a briar patch and emerged with a thousand scratches and half as many blackberries. After I had wasted another weary day trudging around the community in a vain effort to sell the fruit to already overstocked housewives, my grandmother took pity on me and gave me a dime for my pailful. I earned twenty cents more by gathering and selling, for firewood kindling, pine knots and resinous hearts of rotten pine logs, the latter called "lightard" (lightwood). I was able to sell only two sackfuls, because the summer demand was small.

My best source of income was a by-product of romance in the village. There were no private telephones then in Grayson, and it was the custom of the young men to send notes to the girls of their choice, asking for Saturday and Sunday dates. We younger boys carried the notes; the standard payment was a nickel for a trip of up to half a mile and a dime for any longer distance. We always read the notes, of course, but they were unrewardingly dull and identical: "May I have the pleasure of calling upon you this evening [afternoon]?" The formal answers were tritely the same, too: "I shall be pleased to have you call this evening."

Although competition was sharp, I managed to be a courier of love five Sundays in a row, never to the same girl but three times for the same swain, a real rakehell of eighteen. All these errands were nickel routes. By midsummer, then, I had laid away a total of fifty-five cents, and with only forty-five cents to go I was already winding that Ingersoll.

Unhappily for me, there came a recession. The young fellow who played the field, my steadiest customer in the note-carrying business, left town to take a job in Monroe, and at the same time most of the regular dating couples in Grayson apparently reached understandings that obviated the formality of exchanging notes. The blackberry season was over and had been unproductive anyway. It was too early to gather hickory nuts, which might have brought ten cents a bushel.

Several weeks went by, during which I could not add another nickel to my hoard. Then, one afternoon I was scuffing moodily in the back yard near the well, debating whether to blow the whole fifty-five cents on some frivolity, such as a four-bladed knife, when the Miracle happened. On a slick, damp spot off to one side I saw a half dollar. Despite the deep shade cast by an overhanging fig tree, it shone there on the dark ground, looking large as a full moon to me. Rain had fallen a couple of days before, but there was no speck of silt to mar its bright surface. I even remember the date of coinage—1902, the year of my birth, a happy omen, I thought.

Excited, I ran into the house to show my find to my grandparents. A moment later, I understood for the first time what it means to be under suspicion from someone near and dear. Grandpa took the half dollar for safekeeping and began to question me closely, while my grandmother slipped wordlessly away to the kitchen. I led my grandfather out to the back yard and showed him the exact spot where the coin had lain. I fancied I could see the imprint of it still there, but he said he couldn't. Grandma came out. Grandpa asked her a cryptic question, the meaning of which did not escape me, and she shook her head and smiled. . . . She had checked the contents of her teacup bank!

"Don't you believe me?" I cried in despair.

"I believe you, Son," Grandpa said gravely. "You understand, of course, that we must make every effort to find the person who lost the money."

That effort was a strain on my endurance and on my grandfather's limited capacity as a detective. The only visitor at our house, as far as we knew, in the two days since it had rained had been an impecunious and shiftless carpenter. To my joy, he unequivocally disclaimed ownership of the fifty-cent piece. "Didn't have a dime in my jeans that day," he told Grandpa. "I was hoping to borrow a dollar off you—remember—to get some medicine for the baby, but you told me you didn't have a cent on you."

It was possible, of course, that in spite of its shininess the coin had been under the tree by the well before the rain, so my grandfather, taking no chances, wrote to Aunt Effie, who had visited us two weeks earlier. She replied that she had not lost any money, to her knowledge.

It seemed to me that that should have ended the search, but Grandpa waited several more days, on the possibility that someone might come forward to claim the half dollar, or some other clue might come to light. Finally, he solemnly handed it to me, with a little homily on the virtue of honesty and the immorality of the old saying, "Finders, keepers."

The mystery was never cleared up. The only explanation that ever occurred to me was that the carpenter, who was a drinking man, had actually lost the fifty-cent piece and knew it, but didn't want to admit that he had lied to my grandfather about being broke and needing a dollar to buy medicine for his child. He probably wanted enough for a quart of liquor instead of a vial of medicine.

At any rate, I bought the Dollar Ingersoll. With the extra five cents, I got a paper of safety pins. Linked together, they made what I thought was a fine watch chain, which I stretched from the timepiece in that little front pocket of my short pants around to the barlow knife in my right hip pocket.

Thereafter, when we sat on the porch of evenings, watching the sunset and listening to appropriate fiddle music, I would consult my Ingersoll every few minutes, and finally announce importantly:

"Southbound's due."

Grandpa, who didn't have to be told, would smile and nod to himself:

"It is late," he would say.

I suspect he may have been thinking of other things than the southbound.

# V

As I have mentioned, Grandpa tried to be impartial in the Blackman patronage of the Grayson merchants, except for the one gesture to throw as much trade as possible to poor Mr. Roark. But he made one exception in the purchase of what he personally regarded as the most important of all staples that had to be store-bought because it not only could not be grown on our place but had to be imported from a foreign land. That product was coffee, and in buying our regular supply he favored Mixon's. Mr. Mixon courted this trade by stocking not only several kinds of coffee beans in a row of bins but chicory as well.

Chicory is a plant I never saw in its natural state, but it is commonly grown in Europe, Asia, and America—certainly in that part of Louisiana east of the Mississippi River known since 1810 as the Florida Parishes, and no doubt in all the Creole and Cajun country west and south of New Orleans. Grandpa had spent his youth in St. Helena, one of the Floridas, with his elder brothers, Zach and Charles, and his sisters, Alice and Eliza. They were all children of that restless damyankee Zachariah Blackman the First, who came over from England's Cornwall as a youth about 1820, settled somewhere in New York and married a lass named Octavia, a descendant on her mother's side from a pioneer family named Grennan.

It is recorded that Zachariah Blackman I had moved south and settled near Greenburg in St. Helena Parish for reasons Grandpa either never knew or cared too little about to remember; and for equally obscure reasons had moved halfway upstate to Catahoula Parish by the time Grandpa was permitted to straggle home at twenty in defeat from the Civil War. (Pardon, I mean the War Between the States.) There he married Margaret Jane Hodges, and eventually became the owner of his own plantation while rearing his own sizable family, all of whom (except my father) fared well.

Grandpa brought with him to Manifest and to Grayson a cultivated taste for strong coffee blended with a mite of the dried root of the chicory plant, an admixture probably favored by the Creole French, whose Gallic ancestors used chicory as a substitute for coffee. I can't imagine anyone drinking a chicory brew straight; a very little of it adds a piquant touch to coffee, but too much gives it a taste not quite bitter but not like coffee, either.

Grandpa had inherited or developed a formula that pleased

him, but I never learned it, since I never became as finicky about blending coffee (only about the brewing) as he was, and I could take chicory or leave it alone. He bought from Albert Mixon several pounds each of two or three kinds of coffee from South America, plus a smidgen of chicory stocked almost exclusively for him, and Grandma did the parching once a week in our wood-burning kitchen stove. (I know the correct word is "roasting," but coffee was parched, like corn, in our house.)

Coffee-parching days were something to remember, because of the fragrance, which was much stronger and more pervasive than the scent of coffee being brewed over a campfire on a frosty morning. (Some beverages and comestibles smell even better than they taste, among them being properly dripped coffee, rare vintage wines, and slowly fried bacon.)

Grandma used a square tin pan about three inches deep, and she chose a time for the supply replenishing task between breakfast and dinner, or between the noon meal and supper, when the fire only had to be built up a little. During the parching, she had to open the oven door several times to stir the browning beans, and from them arose such smoke that the uninitiated surely would have thought they were burning. And from them there came also an aroma so irresistible that I could not stay away from the kitchen during the hour required for the job. It was as indescribable as it was tantalizing, and promised much more than it yielded in the way of savory satisfaction.

When the green beans had browned to the precise color and brittleness acceptable to Grandma's practiced eye, they were put away in a canister kept on a special shelf behind the stove. Someone's chore right after supper each evening, often mine, was to grind just enough coffee for the next day's use for a family of four. The grinding was done in one of those coffee mills that look like a little house with a handle that goes around horizontally. There was a hopper at the top, with a triangular, slanting metal door that slid back inside to make an aperture just large enough to admit a handful of beans without spilling. A button at the handle hub regulated the fineness of the grounds, which Grandpa preferred to be a little below medium. A drawer pulled all the way out at the bottom of the mill, holding the grounds that were emptied into a covered can.

It was not until I left home that I confirmed through experience something only read about—that it was desirable or even permissible to have a cup of coffee with a meal, even breakfast; or immediately after lunch and dinner. A routine in our house that my grandparents had brought up from St. Helena Parish called for coffee at dawn, at ten o'clock in the morning, and at three o'clock in the afternoon. Elsewhere, I learned later, some people often wake up with a cup just before breakfast, and the between-meals occasions are now called coffee breaks and are so universal as to be fringe benefits provided for in some labor contracts. But drinking coffee at these times does not preclude more with meals; *we* never, never had it with food or just after eating. Unthinkable. At mealtimes, one could drink sweet milk, buttermilk, even clabber with a bit of sugar or cane syrup sweetening—or just plain old well water. No coffee, except at the properly prescribed pick-me-up periods.

Our waking cupfuls were prepared always by Grandpa, who arose at the first streak of daylight ("Night is for sleeping"), whatever the season.

Now and then, when pressed for time, he would permit Grandma to make the midmorning or midafternoon brews, but it seemed to me he never wholeheartedly enjoyed his cupful on those occasions. He gulped quickly and departed.

The ritual of brewing and serving the morning coffee was strictly his prerogative and his sole culinary accomplishment. His last act before going to bed was to set the stage in the kitchen for the coffee bit the next morning.

He would fill a cloth container in the drip pot with a precise amount of coffee he considered necessary for the desired strength of the beverage. Then he would put into an iron kettle with a proboscidiform spout enough well water to make four cups, plus a small extra amount for absorption by the grounds ("one for the pot"). The kettle fitted snugly into a circular eye on the stove from which the lid had been removed, so its bottom would come into direct contact with the flames.

Directly under the kettle in this miniature furnace extending across the front of the stove he would build a complicated little pen of combustibles consisting of dry corncobs, lightard, and seasoned chips of sweet gum, oak, or hickory.

When dawn gave the signal, Grandpa, already awake but still "resting," would pad out to the kitchen in the long drawers he slept in winters and summers (but exchanged for a different pair for day wear), and touch the flame of a long match to the methodically constructed tinderbox. By the time he returned to the bedroom to don his shabby workaday costume, the kettle was beginning to burble softly.

With the first wisp of steam from the spout, he would lift the kettle, replace the eyelid, and set the kettle on it, so that the water would continue to simmer. Violently bubbling water, in his opinion, made coffee taste flat.

Thereafter the brewing was a simple but not hasty process. He would hold the pot under the spout, tip the kettle forward, and permit one or two spoonfuls of water to trickle through a metal sieve overlying the cloth container of grounds. He would set the pot beside the kettle on the stove and listen until the drip ceased. Then would follow other spurts of water and repeated periods of dripping until the kettle was empty and the pot full. He would then refill the kettle to provide hot water for kitchen use.

Among the most vivid of my memories is that of being awakened shortly after dawn with a gentle shake by Grandpa, who would murmur, "Morning coffee, Son." I would sit upright, less than half awake, and reach for the saucer holding a steaming cup. Grandpa would set the kerosene lamp he had brought from the kitchen on my bedside table, light mine for replacement, and then return to the kitchen to take a cup each, one at a time, to Grandma and Sis in their beds.

Having served the rest of us, Grandpa would return to a chair beside the kitchen table and sip his own cupful with an enjoyment that was sometimes audible in our bedrooms. He was unconcerned with the manners of slurping, arguing that the sound both increased and expressed his enjoyment.

In our tender years, my sister and I were given little more than a tasty mixture of sugar and whole milk flavored with coffee. As we grew older, the dosage of caffeine was gradually increased, and my pride of maturity was boundless on the morning I was offered a cup of pure black beverage, with the option of sugar if I wanted it sweet. I did.

On winter mornings, while Grandpa was relishing his coffee in the warm kitchen, I had one inside chore to perform before I was expected to join him in finishing the outside ones. My job was to light the logs I had laid the night before in one of the two back-to-back fireplaces that shared a common chimney. From the time I was old enough to lift a stick of firewood of average size, I knew what many city dwellers never learn: that at least three sticks are required to create a draft and set a wood fire to blazing brightly and giving off sparks and heat. I always laid three for starters and added others later.

It was a cinch to start the morning fire, but it was almost impossible for me to leave it once it was going good and turning dry wood into coals that could be poked with satisfying spurts of flame and smoke. There was something then about a wood fire that set me to daydreaming and made me unconscious of the passage of time. Grandpa would come in after an hour or so, the morning chores all done, to find me sitting in front of the fire, dressed except for one of the pair of black ribbed stocking worn with my short pants, and shoes, gazing into the coals and flames, my thoughts far away from such prosaic activities as separating the milked cow from the calf and pasturing both or bringing in stove wood for the day. He would look at me and shake his head.

"There's a time and place for thinking," he would chide me, "but sitting in front of a morning fire isn't the place and before breakfast isn't the time. Finish dressing, will you, and get out so your grandmother and sister can dress in front of the fire. You might poke up the fire in the kitchen stove for breakfast cooking."

Breakfast, a couple of hours after daylight, usually was a rather hearty meal—hominy grits topped by fried eggs, with thick slices of bacon or smoked ham; and hot buttered biscuits with sugar cane syrup (mistakenly called molasses up north; that blackstrap stuff is the residue from the manufacture of sugar from cane, and is fit only for mixing with grain as animal feed). To wash down the breakfast, one could have any farm beverage he chose—except coffee.

When the sun in the sky told us it was midmorning, we all converged upon the house from wherever we might be working or playing, for the second cup of coffee that day. To heat water for this, Grandpa usually had only to stir the coals that had been banked with ashes after breakfast and add a few sticks of seasoned stove wood. This break usually lasted only about fifteen minutes, then back to whatever we had been doing. For Sis and me, of course, there was no coffee other than the wakeup cupfuls for five days a week during the eight months school was in session. But in summertime and on weekends we joined our grandparents for the 10 A.M. stimulant, which was repeated exactly at midafternoon. No food of any kind was ever consumed with the coffee.

Dinner, the coffeeless main meal of the daily three, was served bountifully right at midday. Our dining room table was a long one, seemingly able to accommodate not only the four of us but any extra number of persons who happened to be present at mealtime.

Deep, oblong china dishes were set at intervals along the cloth-covered table. These were filled with peas, string beans, okra, squash, beets, turnip greens or collards in the spring and late fall, scraped kernels of field corn cooked in milk and butter at green-shuck time. The tender young corn, not to be confused with sweet corn grown in gardens, was called roasnears (roasting ears, though never roasted). The vegetables were cooked fresh in season or emptied from glass Mason jars and heated at other times; and not all of the garden produce named was put on the table at one meal, although it seemed so at times.

Always there was a big bowl of boiled rice, even when Grandma cooked Irish potatoes or yams, called sweet potatoes if they were whitish instead of yellow. I never ate a main meal until I was grown that didn't include rice, which was grown abundantly in the prairie land of southwest Louisiana, as cane was grown in the Sugar Bowl south of New Orleans.

I also never concluded dinner or supper in those days in any other way than with a lavishly buttered biscuit doused with the inevitable cane syrup. The first thing I did at the beginning of the meal was to slice open a biscuit, spread both halves with rich butter, and put it to one side of my plate to soak while I was eating the main course. It then became a sort of dessert. At supper, I ate the biscuit buttered and syrupy, but cold.

This may be blasphemy, but I wasn't too fond of Grandma's regular baking powder biscuits that she made from dough kneaded in a wooden tray just before they were put into the oven. Too thick and not too fluffy. But I've never tasted any bakery product so delicious as her sourdough ones. These were prepared in the same way in the afternoon, then allowed to sour in a pan overnight. Instead of rising, they baked flat and crisp, with spots like freckles on top, and rich, brown bottom-crusts.

We had fresh meat for dinner only during hog-killing time in the first cold spell of winter. Weekdays, there were plenty of chunks of fat meat, called sowbelly by some, cooked with the vegetables to season them, but I couldn't swallow the sickening stuff. (Grandpa loved it, Grandma just ate it, Sis nibbled at it.) Sundays, there was sometimes cured meat, but most often chicken cooked in one form or another; and I got so surfeited that I could hardly stand the sight of fowl. I still can't.

One curious custom I have never encountered elsewhere was the setting of the table with the plates turned upside down on the tablecloth and flanked by the cutlery. After Grandpa returned thanks ("asked the blessing" was our phrase), each of us turned over his plate and began filling it as the dishes of food were passed. Grandpa mumbled when he asked the blessing, and I never could quite hear what he was saying; he wasn't speaking for our benefit, but talking privately to God. And although I had been able to read since before memory, I just never happened to look at the words in the circles on the back of the dinner plates. I was past ten when I discovered the words imprinted and baked there were a trademark and not the ones Grandpa was reading to himself and to his Deity.

Supper was a hasty, unimportant meal of cold and unappetizing leftovers, with occasionally a dish of fruit in season or jam of some kind to supplant the syrup, or follow it, on the cold biscuits. Sometimes after we got an icebox we drank tall glasses of iced tea, heavily sugared. There never was coffee for supper, either.

I had watched Grandpa so often as he made the midmorning and midafternoon coffee that I was sure I knew precisely how to do it myself. One dark and early morning in summertime, I was inspired to try it, before going on a squirrel hunt in the river hills with Brownie. He was a neighbor boy across the railroad tracks who was my good friend most of the time, my enemy now and then, and my rival always.

I had received a single-barrel shotgun when I was quite young as a gift from my Uncle Milton, the youngest of Grandpa's children. Grandpa did not voice his disapproval, but I felt it. He nevertheless taught me how to carry and otherwise handle it safely, but I was pretty sure he hoped I would tire of it soon. I did, chiefly because I was such a poor marksman I could never hit anything except a sitting quail now and then.

On this particular morning, Brownie whistled me out of bed a good hour before dawn, and after I was dressed I became aware (as did Brownie) that I was irritable and lacking in enthusiasm for the hunt. Presently it dawned on me that the cause was the lack of the usual warming, aromatic, soothing cup of coffee upon awaking and arising. A daring thought occurred to me: I would make the coffee myself; not only that, I would surprise Grandpa by taking a cup to *his* bed as a wake-up gesture in appreciation of the many, many such similar favors on his part in the past.

While my bored non-coffee-drinking friend Brownie watched impatiently, I inspected Grandpa's overnight preparations in the kitchen and set about the brewing of coffee as though I had done it all my life. I touched a match to the fat pine, and it caught fire immediately. The corncobs blazed, the chips began to crackle. In a remarkably short time, the kettle began to spurt a thin column of steam, and I started the pouring and dripping process.

When the coffee was made, I poured a cupful, added sugar, and sampled it. It tasted fine.

"Want a cup?" I asked Brownie.

"No," he said, grumbling. "Never drink the stuff. Don't like it. Let's get going, so we can make the hills by first light."

"Just a minute," I said, finishing my cup. "I'm gonna take a cup in to Grandpa."

My grandfather sat up quickly, startled, as I approached his bed with the lamp and the cup of coffee on a tray, the bowl of sugar and a pitcher of milk alongside for him to suit his own taste. . . . Grandma and Sis were asleep in the next room.

"Got up early to go hunting," I said in an offhand manner, "so I made the coffee myself. Thought I'd bring in a cup for you, for a change."

He looked at me blankly for a moment, then smiled with understanding and affection. "Why, that's mighty thoughtful of you, Son," he said. He added milk and sugar, raised the cup to his lips, sipped and smacked. "Fine coffee," was his verdict, and I sighed with relief. "Mighty fine coffee. You sure got the touch, my boy." After a couple more swallows, he set the cup down on the saucer.

"You know," he said almost to himself, "this is the first time in my life I ever had a cup of coffee in bed. Feels sort of peculiar."

Since he made no move to lift the cup again, I said diffidently, "Well, guess I'll be going."

He smiled at me again and said, "Be careful. You can be sure the squirrels will. And thanks for the coffee. Thanks for a new experience."

I left him sitting there in bed, thoughtfully holding the cup again but not drinking from it. I decided it was a bit too early to wake Grandma and Sis, so my impatient friend and I set out for the hunting territory. But as we passed the barn, I noticed I had less than half a box of shells in my hunting bag, and, to Brownie's disgust, I told him to wait while I ran back to the house to get more.

As I entered the kitchen noiselessly on bare feet, Grandpa looked up guiltily from a position beside the stove. He was stirring the ashes, adding new chips, and obviously about to put water to boil for a new potful of coffee. Mine had been poured out. He was embarrassed for a moment, but he was never long at a loss for words.

"Don't feel bad, Son," he urged. "It's me and my habits, not you. You made a mighty fine cup of coffee. As I said, you really have the touch. But I been doing this so long I just can't start the day without making my own coffee."

I suppose I still looked a little hurt and uncomprehending, because he continued explaining, "It's like this: there never was a cup of coffee half so good as the pleasure of making it and the anticipation of drinking it. You handed me a cupful out of the blue—or, I should say, out of the dark—and caught me unawares. I just can't enjoy coffee without the anticipation."

I was sure my coffee was as good as his, but I never again deprived him of his well-earned right of coffee anticipation.

# VI

---

Acquisition of that shotgun just before my first teen year ended a feud and rivalry between my sister and me that began when we were quite young. The first sibling controversies were over our ages and what to call each other. I was a little more than eighteen months older than she, and naturally lorded it over her for that reason. But my superiority in this respect did not remain constant, since we did not think in terms of half years. On her March 6 birthday each year, she triumphantly pointed out that she was now only a year younger than I, and I needn't act so smartypants. Then, when my September 29 natal day rolled around, I crowed that I was now two years her senior and should be accorded the respect that was thus my due—not in those words, of course. We bickered endlessly over this.

Then, the matter of names: Our grandparents always called me Son, never Marion except on the occasions when Grandma was calling me home from somewhere within the range of her voice—and then it was two long, not unmusical syllables: "Mer—y-o-o-o-n!" My sister was Maude or Maudie to her grandparents. She copied Grandpa and Grandma in calling me "Son," but I wouldn't permit such impertinence from someone my junior, and a girl at that. I cured her by addressing her and referring to her as "Daughter." She definitely did not care for that, so I soon became just "Brother" to her, shortened in writing to "Bro." I reverted to "Sis," which became and still is my name for her.

Sis was always a tiny thing—"no bigger than a minute" was a commonly used description. Her physical development was normal in other respects but she never tipped the scales over a hundred pounds through all the stages of adolescence, college years, marriage, children, and grandchildren. I paid scant attention to her growth from child to woman, being more interested in older girls not related to me at that stage. Sis had soft, expressive brown eyes, and I would say she really was a pretty girl, but no male is a dependable judge of beauty in his sister or his wife.

I suppose most boys who arrogantly assume superiority over younger sisters solely on the basis of masculinity and seniority make life miserable for them by bullying and teasing; I was no exception. She didn't take it meekly. Small and skinny as she was, she was wiry, tough, and she could retaliate vindictively. She fought back with the best weapons she had, fingernails and tattletales, and I often got scars from both.

One school day, for example, when we had come home for the noonday meal, she announced so casually as to sound guileless:

"Brother got in trouble at school today."

"What kind of trouble?"

"Oh, I don't know just what happened," Sis said, not even looking at me or our grandparents. "Something to do with a girl," she added vaguely.

Grandpa merely looked thoughtful, but Grandma directed at me such a wounded, accusing look that I fled from the table feeling disgraced. Her expression told me—or I so interpreted it—that she suspected I had been guilty of unimaginable and unforgivable acts of molestation or vulgarity involving some hapless little girl; and had been caught at it and punished by the teacher. A juvenile sex fiend, no less.

It was at once too involved and too simple to explain that my offense had been clownish rather than sexual.

What actually happened—and I was bitterly certain that Sis knew it—was that in some sort of student march into the auditorium I had been paired accidentally with a girl named Clara who was my age but a head taller. She was sensitive about this and I had in me a streak of meanness, as most children have. So, acting the buffoon, I leaned over to one side as low as I could and peered up at her as we marched along as though asking the hoary and unfunny question often directed at tall people: "How's the weather up there?"

As I had hoped and expected, this convulsed my fellow students (who had mean streaks too, of course). But the teacher was no more amused than poor Clara; she seized me by an ear and hustled me to the end of the line where I completed the march in deserved isolation.

That was all there was to the incident, but thanks to my sly sister's account of it, involving no outright falsehood that I could pin down, Grandma was convinced I had been guilty of more than simple misbehavior. I really hated my sister then. However, my grandparents never brought up the subject again, and they probably concluded that if anything serious had occurred they would have heard about it directly from the school authorities.

Sis won that round, which no doubt was in retaliation for some sort of humiliation or indignity to which I had subjected her (I remember her cruelties better than mine). We fought often, sometimes physically, but more often with words, and I can still hear my grandmother's recurrent plaint, "I hope and pray that you two will learn some day to be good and kind to each other."

Sis was not a real tomboy and I wasn't a sissy, but we were copycats in our sibling rivalry; each had to do what the other did. I seem to recall that she bested me oftener than I triumphed over her.

Grandpa taught me how to build a pyramid-shaped bird trap of slats requiring the minimum use of carpenter tools, since neither of us was very skilled with them. Sis watched, then made her own trap—and caught more birds than I did. She promptly set them all free without troubling to band them herself or to let me do it.

When I learned to ride a bicycle, a borrowed one, she swiped it behind my back and mastered that skill, too; but she rode it so recklessly that she cracked up, damaging the machine. I had to pay for the repairs out of my very limited savings, thus delaying my acquisition of a second-hand bike for myself.

I invaded her field of activities, too. I duplicated her efforts to learn some of the arts of cooking until Grandma chased both of us out of the kitchen. Sis took up crocheting, with Grandma instructing her in the use of steel needles with ordinary cotton thread and bone ones for wool yarn. I watched, and learned the single stitch, the double stitch, and the technique of turning and following patterns. I sneaked some thread and a steel needle from her sewing basket once and crocheted a doily that I entered anonymously in the parish fair in Columbia. It actually won an honorable mention, which made Sis furious; her entry was passed over entirely by the judges.

(A quarter of a century later, my wife and her mother were astonished when they came home from shopping one day to find me sitting in the living room, with a drink on a convenient table, competently finishing in two colors of wool yarn one of those cold-weather caps for boys, complete with turned-up brim and pompom. My son liked it fine, but he was too canny ever to mention to his pals that Daddy had made it.)

Then I got the shotgun.

Grandpa taught me to handle it properly, but Sis knew better than to ask him for instructions, and of course Brownie and I refused to take her along on our bird and squirrel hunts.

But she kept pestering me to let her fire the gun, and I finally gave in, even though I was pretty certain she wasn't going to enjoy the experience. My single-barrel, twelve-gauge, choke-bore gun was light of weight, and when a black-powder shell was discharged in it, the recoil had a force like the kick of a mule. I was short of stature but fairly sturdy and well-muscled, but to absorb the shock when the gun went off, I had to press the stock firmly against the right shoulder and stand with one leg braced behind the other. Since Sis was so much lighter and unaware of the staggering thrust—well, I warned her:

"All right, all right," I said. "You're not big enough nor strong enough to handle a shotgun, but if you're stubborn and stupid enough to try, let's go."

I took her out to the Near Pasture, loaded the gun, gingerly cocked it while holding it pointed away from both of us, put it to her right shoulder, guided her left hand forward to the barrel and her right to the guarded trigger, and indicated a field sparrow perched on a weed fifty feet away.

"Go ahead," I ordered. "Shoot. Shoot to kill."

Sis already had learned somehow the technique of aiming. She brought the gun up waveringly, peered along the barrel through the rear sight with her right eye, lined up the target with the front sight, then steadied the weapon as best she could, and pulled he trigger.

As I had anticipated and even wickedly planned, the blast of the gun held loosely against her shoulder smacked against her collarbone like a battering ram and sent her tumbling backassward and head over heels on the ground.

She wasn't hurt and she quickly scrambled to her feet, dropping the gun which she had clung to in her back somersault. Instead of yelling at me, she ran forward to the weed where the bird had been perching.

It now lay on the ground, very dead and looking more like a fistful of tousled and gory feathers than a field sparrow. Her aim at her first shotgun target had been perfect, the result irremediable. Sis burst into tears.

"Oh, the poor little thing," she sobbed.

Then and there she used a sharp stick to dig a shallow grave in the loose turf and buried the bird. After she had smoothed the tiny mound and placed a twig of the weed as a headstone, she turned a baleful glare in my direction and made a comment I didn't understand then, and don't yet.

"You and your dad-gummed crocheting!"

It may have been just coincidental with approaching teen-age and mutual tolerance, but our rivalry in boy-versus-girl competition ended that day. Thereafter, she went her own feminine way and I followed my masculine pursuits, with neither of us insisting on copying the other. We let each other alone; we stopped quarreling and fighting; she quit bearing tales and I refrained from teasing and bullying. We got along together just fine.

Grandma observed this cessation of hostilities and continued peace with wonder and disbelief at first and then with increasing satisfaction.

"At last," she sighed one evening as we all sat peacefully on the porch waiting for the southbound. "I was beginning to fear I'd never live to see the day when you two would be good and kind to each other. Thank God."

"Oh, come now, Mother," Grandpa chided her gently, "you should have known these things always work themselves out. Remember how it was with our first brood? It was three boys against four girls then, and they not only took sister-brother sides, but had descending-age pecking order among all of them, from Robert right down to Milton."

Our peace actually was marked by something more significant than the usual brother-sister blood-kin affection, a new relationship that occurs far too seldom in families: We were good friends. We still are.

# VII

---

Most of my memories of Grayson thus far have dwelt upon summer happenings, but there was an unmistakable wintertime in northern Louisiana and a few cold-weather activities worth recalling. Most Northerners have the mistaken impression that Louisiana is semitropical, like southernmost Florida. While the year-round mean temperature for southern Louisiana is above sixty-eight degrees (fifty-five for January and eighty-two for August), the figures for northern Louisiana are several degrees lower, with a January average of forty-eight. I seldom saw snow in my youth, though light falls were reported once or twice as far south as Baton Rouge and even New Orleans on one historic occasion, but winter sleet and ice storms were not uncommon in Grayson in midwinter. On more than one morning, I awoke to a glittering world of bare tree limbs encased in crystal, and had to break thin ice in the back-porch water bucket and washbasin. Fireplace heat was required during at least three months of the twelve, longer in some years.

Mention of fireplaces inevitably suggests chimneys, with Santa descending them on Christmas Eve with a pack of good-ies for deserving children to find in their stockings tacked to the mantelpiece when they awoke bright-eyed and bushy-tailed on Christmas morning. (I was not long fooled by this pretty fable, because our chimney seemed too small and it forked into two separate fireplaces in different rooms. Even to my childish mind, this seemed to present St. Nick with an insuperable physical barrier or to require an irrevocable deci-sion with a fifty-fifty chance of being wrong. Besides, when I was about seven, I happened to be still awake one Christmas Eve to see dimly an impatient and sleepy grandfather filling two limply hanging stockings. But I pretended innocent belief in the deception as long as it seemed reasonable.)

There were a few other Yuletide joys that come vividly to mind, among them one custom that was peculiar to that sec-tion of the South, or perhaps only to northern Louisiana. Fireworks were always set off at Christmastime, never on the Fourth of July or any other occasion.

Every remembered Christmas Eve of my youth, keen com-petition developed among a couple of my young neighbors and me to see whose fireworks could produce not the most arresting visual display but the most noise. At that time, Roman candles were so expensive as to be rare and the cost of rockets also was prohibitive. Firecrackers were the thing.

The smallest ones, at the time of the Christmas contest I remember best, were the red Chinese one-inchers that came in five-cent packets of twenty or thirty, with interwoven fuses. The two-, four-, and six-inchers were sold in thin cardboard boxes that cost, respectively, five, ten, and fifteen cents each and contained ten, eight, or five red crackers.

The big ones, the yellow eight-inch cannons, were not available that Christmas in Grayson, but could be bought in Columbia, at the staggering cost of twenty-five cents each. It was reported that ten-inch supercannons could be purchased for fifty cents in Monroe. Firearms, which some people used to celebrate Christmas, didn't count in our competition. The roaring boom of shotguns and the trailing crack of rifles were too familiar the year around, and it didn't require keen ears to distinguish them from firecrackers.

My rivals that year were my cousin Malcolm Grayson, who was spending the holiday next door at the home of his Grandfather Grayson, and Brownie, my friendly enemy who lived across the railroad tracks from us.

When Malcolm came to Grayson, he seldom stayed with us. His Grandpa Grayson appeared more affluent and was more indulgent than our mutual Grandpa Blackman, who had little liking for wasteful fripperies and none for noise.

I had good reason, then, to fear that Malcolm would be loaded for the firecracker contest, which was to take place soon after dark. I also knew that Brownie, whose father was a well-to-do small sawmill owner, would be amply supplied. My limited Yuletide budget allowed only seventy-five cents for fireworks, and I couldn't see how I would be able to hold my own against them.

I was brooding aloud about this one day a couple of weeks before Christmas while I was helping Grandpa gather a slide-load of pine knots in the wooded part of the Back Forty. I hoped he might be able to let me have an extra dollar, or at least suggest ways I might yet earn such a sum. He nodded in his preoccupied way while I explained my problem and the humiliation I would suffer if I should be outbanged too badly by Brownie and Malcolm, especially the latter. I suspected, without any evidence to support the thought, that my grandfather was not too fond of Cousin Malcolm; at any rate, I hoped he was fonder of me than of a grandson who preferred another grandfather.

Finally, after we started for the house with our load, he gave me his full attention and asked, "The main objective is noise, right?"

"Sure," I said eagerly, "but it's got to be explosive noise. Not just clatter, and not guns."

"Turn in here," he suddenly directed.

I turned Old Black into a trail that led to Hurricane Creek, which wound through our property. For a quarter of a mile, at this point, both banks were lined with thick stands of bamboo canes, as straight as fence pickets and some of them more than twenty feet tall. They made splendid fishing poles.

"Cut down three or four of those," Grandpa ordered.

I was bursting to ask questions, but I knew better. I took an axe from the slide and cut down four canes of fairly good size. When I brought them over, I found my grandfather had started a hot fire of pine knots. It was a clear, cold day, and the fire felt good. When it reached its peak, Grandpa picked up one of the canes by the small end and thrust the bottom joint into the fire. I watched, fascinated.

"Stand back, Son," he said. I stood back.

Suddenly he lifted the large end of the cane pole high into

the cold air. There was an explosion that either knocked my cap off or startled me into jumping out from under it. The noise was equivalent to that of a good eight-incher, if I ever heard one. Grandpa, smiling, lowered the cane, and I saw that it was split nearly half its length.

"How'd you do that?" I demanded excitedly. "What caused that?"

He explained that the heat of the fire vaporized the sap still remaining in the cane between the joints, each section sealed off from the next, and that the sudden hoist into cold air had produced the explosion. I suppose there is some explanation in physics for this, but if he knew it he didn't tell me; I wasn't interested in the technicalities, anyway, just in the wonderful effect.

"Now you try it," he suggested.

Somewhat fearfully, I seized a cane and poked the large end into the fire. Grandpa watched intently, and I looked at him for a signal.

"Now!" he said.

I responded too tardily. Before I could jerk the cane into the air, there was a hissing sound, and I saw that the bottom joint had quietly come apart, allowing the vaporized sap to escape.

"You got to watch it closely," he explained. "When it first begins to shrivel and to curl a little, that's the time to give it the cold-air treatment. Fast."

I followed his directions on the next attempt and was rewarded with a wildly satisfying explosion. The fourth cane also shattered loudly, and I snatched up the axe.

"Not now," Grandpa said. "Time for coffee." He then asked, "Does that give you any notions for Christmas?"

"It sure does," I said happily. "Oh, boy!"

From then on until the holiday, I went every day to Hurricane Creek (at a point as far away from town as possible), built a fire, and practiced.

I learned several things. One, which worried me, was that cold air was absolutely essential. On a mild day, to be expected occasionally even in midwinter, nothing happened when the heated bamboo was thrust aloft. No explosion. Nothing. Another, which excited me, was that it wasn't necessary to use a whole cumbersome cane to get an explosion. Thereafter, I took along a handsaw and cut the canes into lengths, each with a sealed space between joints and a handhold of half or three-quarters of another. With cotton gloves on, I could hold such a length of cane in the fire, wait for it to begin shriveling and curling, and then hurl it high into the air, where it would burst. This technique not only made the explosive devices easier to handle, but gave me a range in decibels in each cane, comparable to puny two-inchers at the small end and ranging up to cannons at the large end—the like of which I had never heard measured in firecracker inches. . . . I stored up a supply of munitions and hoped for a cold spell.

The weather turned perfect for my purpose on Christmas Eve. After first-dark, it was a chill, starlit night, presaging frost. I built a hot oakwood fire on our front lawn, off to one side away from my pin oak, and waited for the opening sound-off from my rivals.

Across the railroad tracks, Brownie started it, with a packet of one-inch Chinese, set off in a fusillade. Next door, Malcolm followed suit. Then—contemptuously, I'm afraid—I fired a similar packet. That was the custom. Five cents it cost me. Then the boys began bringing up their heavier artillery. . . . I reached toward the first of my piles of carefully sorted lengths of cane.

Well, it was a rout. When either or both of them set off two-inchers or larger ones, I topped them by countering with a salvo of bamboo joints at least twice as loud. I shot six to their one, having learned by practice to keep several lengths heating at once, by staggering their insertion into the fire, timed from left to right. I lost a few that way, but the overall result was wonderful.

At last, Malcolm shot a couple of eight-inchers, and Brownie set off three in a row. I had a feeling Brownie was through. There was a long silence. I waited tensely for the next explosion from Malcolm, and I'm sure that, across the railroad tracks, Brownie did too.

Finally, from the darkness next door, it came! I'd never heard a fabulous ten-incher go off before, but I knew Malcolm's finale must have been one, and that he had persuaded Grandpa Grayson to bring it to him from Monroe. A fifty-center.

A year earlier, I would have thought it devastatingly conclusive; now in my new-found superiority, it was not even impressive. But it was what I had been waiting to hear. I gave Brownie a few more minutes to respond, but as I had expected, he was finished. He had no ten-incher.

I stirred my fire and carefully laid in, a few seconds apart, my two beauties reserved for this moment. The sealed lengths were nearly two feet long and more than an inch in diameter. I watched them closely as they lay in the glowing coals with handholds sticking out toward me.

One curled. I threw it. The other curled. I threw it.

They shattered high in the air, a couple of seconds apart, with such concussion that I thought I felt it even through the ground.

"Lord save us!" Grandpa ejaculated impiously from our dark front porch.

I ran up the steps and dimly saw him standing there with Grandma and Sis.

"Did you hear that, Grandpa?" I cried foolishly. "Did you hear it?"

"Did I hear it!" he exclaimed. "They must have heard it in the next parish." He added thoughtfully. "You're lucky to have any fingers left, throwing short lengths like that."

"Oh, I was careful," I said.

"I was watching," he said.

As I turned to go, he stopped me.

"Here," he said, thrusting two objects at me. "The boys will be coming over, I expect. You may need these to cover up." The three of them went back into the house.

I ran out to the fire and by its waning light saw that what he had given me was two eight-inchers. He must have made a special trip to Columbia to get them!

Brownie and Malcolm soon sidled into the decreasing circle of firelight. Over the embers I was chafing my hands, as though keeping them warm had been the purpose of the fire. (They had used sulfur matches to light the fuses of their firecrackers.) Both boys looked all around but saw nothing that would give me away. The splinters from my fireworks had fallen outside the lighted area, and I had hidden a few leftovers under the porch.

"Pretty good show," Brownie said grudgingly.

"Who got your ten-inchers for you?" Malcolm demanded. "Not Grandpa Blackman, I bet."

"What do you mean, *ten*-inchers?" I retorted scornfully. "Did you ever hear those babies sound like my last round?" I was giving him no information, but plenty to ponder over.

"What I want to know," Brownie said, "is how you shot off those two big ones almost at the same time. That's the way to lose a hand."

"Oh, it's not hard," I said nonchalantly, "if you're—if you're two-handed," I concluded ambiguously.

"You got any more of those big ones?" Malcolm asked suspiciously.

"That's for me to know and you to find out," I said tartly. "Oh, by the way—you guys got anything left to wake up the town with tomorrow morning?" Saving a big firecracker to greet Christmas Day was another custom.

"Not me," Brownie said glumly. "I shot my wad."

"That ten-incher was *my* last," Malcolm admitted.

I then rubbed salt into their wounds of defeat by grandly handing each of them an eight-incher Grandpa had given me.

"Just a couple of medium ones I had left," I said casually. "I won't need them. . . . Well, I got to get to bed. Good night, all. Merry Christmas!"

Let them stay awake all night and wonder, I thought.

As I finished helping Grandpa with the chores (for a change) the next morning, I heard Brownie set off his gift eight-incher. Malcolm soon replied with his. I sauntered out to the front porch steps and waved airily to each of them.

Then, while they waited expectantly for they knew not what, I dismissed them with another gesture and strolled back into the house. Anything after last night would have been an anticlimax. I went into the dining room and ate the breakfast of a champion.

Grandpa Blackman, looking well-pleased with me—and himself—chuckled reminiscently and ate with good appetite, too.

# VIII

———

The mentionable pastimes and pleasures available in a sleepy, ugly, impoverished, unincorporated village such as Grayson in my time were few and unexciting, and it is surprising to recall just how large a role the railroad played in the drab leisure time activities of the residents. The period was before behemoth buses invited travelers to leave the driving to them; privately owned automobiles and trucks were primitive and scarce for the same reason—no good roads; and airplanes, of course, were still just dangerous novelties in the transportation field. Our railroad thus was a sort of Be-All lifeline; it gaveth and it tooketh away, in the sense that it brought many things consumed in various ways, and delivered to the outside world the few things produced for export. It also provided transportation for visitors and departing travelers, both few in number.

But in addition to these practical functions, the railroad and its rolling stock were the nucleus around which most of the community's social life revolved. The morning and evening passenger trains were the most important. The former arrived before the day's work began for most residents, and the latter after it ended. Townspeople of all ages wandered down to the depot (nobody called it a station) to see the trains come in; they noted the identity of the occasional passenger alighting or boarding by means of a hand-carried step provided by the conductor; then as the train left they followed the mail cart to the post office, there to exchange news, gossip, farming and timber information, and just enjoy one another's company until Mr. Seiler called out "All up," and stood by to distribute the postal dividends to his clientele without private mail boxes.

The single railroad track was as popular as Welcome Home Cemetery for Saturday and Sunday afternoon courting by young folks of suitable ages. There were grassy spots available on right-of-way embankments and beside graves, respectively, both out of sight of curious onlookers who were not too brazen voyeurs. Small fry learned the teetering skill of "walking the rails" and used the rock gravel ballast of the roadbed as an inexhaustive supply of ammunition for their slingshots, commonly called "nigger"-shooters with never a thought of the ethnic threat or insult implied in the term. The commonest furtive targets were the green glass insulators on the telegraph poles supporting the wires strung parallel to the track.

The first and most enduring railroad attraction for me was the infinite variety of spine-tingling steam locomotive whistles sounded by the engineers by means of cords extending forward from their side of the cab, on the right. No one who has not lived beside a railroad can ever quite comprehend the spell exerted by a distant locomotive whistle even when heard by day, but more especially in the deep stillness of a small-town night.

They were as varied in decibel and tone as a fine organ's pipes. The deep-throated moans from the larger freight engines made those of the passenger trains, with fewer cars and less weight to pull, sound like anemic whines. Many freight trains passed Grayson each day, and I learned at a very early age to identify the number of each locomotive in regular use by the sound of its whistle.

"That's old Four-fifty-four," I would tell my sister several minutes before it came close enough to read the huge yellow numerals on the sides of the cab. I was seldom wrong, and Sis couldn't have cared less that I was right.

The whistle notes were sounded in short and long blasts, which trainmen designated on paper thusly:

$$\cdot \; — \; —$$

Each combination used had a meaning as a signal, and I came to know these too by ear and observation. Later, I confirmed my interpretations from official charts, but have forgotten most of them.

The whistle signals I remember being used most often by trains in and approaching Grayson on the Iron Mountain Branch of the Missouri Pacific were:

·     Apply brakes, stop

— —     Release brakes, proceed

— · · ·     Flagman, protect rear of train

— — — —     Flagman, return

· · ·     When standing, will back up; when
running, will stop at next station

· · · ·     Call for signals from agent so
train can proceed

— — · —     Approaching public crossing at grade

————     Approaching station

The last two were the most familiar, because both were sounded by every train, passenger or freight, that went through Grayson. Since the grade crossing was just north of the depot in the middle of the town, the order in which the two signals were sounded was reversed by the southbound and northbound trains.

There was one set of haunting whistle sounds borne to my ears every windless evening just before dusk that had no signal meaning for me until Grandpa Blackman explained it. Sometimes it went like this:

· —— — · ———— — ·

Then there would be such variations as

— — — — · —— · · · ————

This mystery was not on the Iron Mountain but on the log train road operated by the Clarks Lumber Company to feed its greedy appetite for pine timber before it exhausted the supply and moved elsewhere. The narrow-gauge line ran through cutover land about two miles west and south of Grayson. The locomotives were smaller than the public carrier's, but the steam whistles certainly seemed larger and louder. The engineers didn't really need whistles for operational signals, because there were no flagmen, no stations, and no grade crossings. Yet the regular driver on the final run at day's end pulled his whistle cord almost continuously for the last mile or so, breaking up the sound into shorts and longs but following no pattern with meaning recognizable by me. It was musical, in the long-ago-and-far-away manner, but I mentioned one evening to Grandpa Blackman that it seemed wasteful of steam and senseless to me.

"Is he just fooling around because he likes the sound of his whistle," I asked, "or is he saying something to somebody?"

"He's saying something, all right," Grandpa replied. "I know that particular last-train-of-the-day engineer, and I asked him about it one Sunday when he was up here for something. He lives with his wife and children in a pretty sorry cabin back in a patch of hardwood trees away from the track through the stumps.

"He's just talking to his wife with that whistle in the last mile on the way home," Grandpa explained. "They've worked out a code of longs and shorts they both understand but nobody else does."

"I wonder what he tells her," I said, fascinated.

"Oh, it's just man-to-wife talk . . . whether it was a good day or a bad day at work . . . what he'd like to have for supper. . . . Maybe he even says he loves her—if he does. Pretty nice arrangement for him; she can't talk back. Probably one of the few such domestic situations in the world," he concluded dryly.

It seemed sort of romantic to me; I thought, my, what a nice, distinctive way to communicate. Thereafter, when I heard that long-drawn log train wail coming from the direction of the sunset, I envisioned a devoted woman wearing a plain housedress with an apron over it in an unpainted cabin in the woods, listening to her man chat about his day and his appetite. This last led to a little sad thought, though. I had heard that the pay for sawmill workers wasn't too generous and he wasn't likely to have much choice for his evening meal. The waiting wife probably would be told only whether he preferred his fat meat fried with grits or boiled with collards and some cornbread to go with it.

Grandpa readily admitted he was an authority on railroads (among many other subjects) and pointed out that his life span covered their period of greatest growth, renown, legend, and influence. When he got started on the subject and had time, he would ramble on endlessly, and I would jot down the facts that interested me soon afterward in a notebook, using a shorthand of my own. I never got around to checking what he told me, because my interest in railroads had waned almost to zero by the time I had attained the age and opportunity for research. However, he read everything on that topic that came his way and he could always remember very accurately most of what he read and heard. Here then are a few "high iron" highlights as he passed them along to me, with emphasis on Louisiana and our own Iron Mountain.

In the seventy years from the trial run of the first steam locomotive in the United States, the English-imported "Sturbridge Lion," somewhere in Pennsylvania, until I was born, pioneer builders had laid 190,000 road miles of standard-gauge (four feet eight and one-half inches) track, crisscrossing the nation. Louisiana had about 2,800 of these miles; they doubled during the decade in which I was born, then began to decline in number and use.

Besides the Iron Mountain, the trackage with which I was then familiar was the Vicksburg, Shreveport and Pacific (change at Monroe to MoPac when traveling from Shreveport to Grayson and vice versa); and the Louisiana and Arkansas Railway extending from a point north and east of Shreveport (change at Georgetown from MoPac) to Utility and Jonesville and thence across the Mississippi by ferry from Vidalia to Natchez. Because of the color of the coach cushions, one of these two carriers we rode to visit our Black Belt relatives was to me the Blue Train and the other the Red Train, but I can't recall which was which.

Grandpa related a lot of information I skipped about federal railroad land grants, started by Illinois Senator Stephen Douglas just ten years before he was defeated by Abe Lincoln in 1860 for the Presidency; but the oft-told story of the meeting of the westward building Union Pacific and the eastward extending Central Pacific was the incident Grandpa dwelt upon most glowingly.

He was only sixteen at the time and thousands of miles away in Catahoula Parish, but to hear him tell it he was right there in the Utah desert when the junction was completed with the laying of a polished California laurel crosstie and the driving of a ceremonial spike of California gold. As usual, he had a quotation and a wry comment. The quote was a quatrain by Bret Harte:

> What was it the engineers said,
> Pilots [da-de-da]* head to head
> Facing on a single track
> Half a world behind each back?

Grandpa's comment: "An interesting topic for speculation, but what I'd really like to know and never could find out is what happened to that gold railroad spike. It's a sure bet it

_____
* *Can't recall that missing word.*

wasn't left there in that polished laurel crosstie, but who got it? The U.P., the C.P., Congress, or the section foreman? Got to look into that angle some day. Somebody must know the answer."

(I recalled the quatrain when I was studying American literature in college and noted two things about Bret Harte: Although he was best known for his stories celebrating the Old West, he was a New Yorker; and he died the year I was born.)

It was another New Yorker, George Jay Gould, born the year Grandpa was dragooned into fighting reluctantly on the Rebel side in the Civil War, who expanded into central Louisiana and elsewhere in the Southwest the railroad empire he inherited from the first Jay Gould (christened Jason) on his father's death in 1892.

Our old Iron Mountain of beloved memory grew out of the extension of two little Gould-owned lines—one from Lake Charles (where Aunt Minnie lived) north to Alexandria; and the other from Alexandria north through Grayson and Monroe to join a connecting link to Little Rock. There a main MoPac line heads southwestward into Texas through the border city of Texarkana.

Even though the Iron Mountain wound up as a mere branch line, its name antedated the Missouri Pacific as a system. In fact, the system's beginning link was built early in the 1850's to bring to market in St. Louis the valuable mineral deposits in Iron Mountain, a community about fifty miles south of the Missouri metropolis. Hence the name of the line.

By the time George Jay Gould had lost most of his railroad holdings, had been sued by other members of the family, and had fled to Menton, France, to die as an expatriate in 1923, I was in college and had lost interest in the Iron Mountain. My railroad then was the Louisiana Railway and Navigation Company, which derived the marine part of its name from an eight-mile downstream ferry crossing of the Mississippi en route from Shreveport to Baton Rouge. Fares on the L.R. & N. were lower than on the Texas and Pacific between the same points, and I chose it for travel back and forth from a summer job in Shreveport to college in Baton Rouge.

Branch line or whatever, the Iron Mountain certainly loomed large in my life during the last half of the first decade and all of the second in the twentieth century.

What boy growing up in a small railroad town, with a single track and a mile-long siding where one freight train "went into the hole" for another to pass in the opposite direction, can forget the thrill of watching a flying switch? It was enacted this way:

When a local freight train from Monroe had to set out a boxcar on a second siding (called "loading") for shipment of lumber, cotton bales, or whatever, the train would stop in front of our house and disconnect the set-out car behind the locomotive tender from the rest of the train. The engineer would start the locomotive toward the siding switch, where one brakeman stood at the manual control. A second rode between the locomotive and the boxcar. At the proper moment, brakeman number two would uncouple the car to let it coast while he climbed to its top to apply the hand brake with a wheel. The locomotive would chuff furiously ahead of the coasting car down the main track. Brakeman number one would let it pass him, then throw the switch to divert the free-gliding car onto the first siding. Then the locomotive would back up, entering the siding, and nuzzle the slowing boxcar onto the loading siding by means of another open switch. Then back to recouple with the rest of the train and continue the journey, after a complex-sounding but simple railroad maneuver. Great show!

Then, there were the Work Trains, which sometimes paused a few days on the loading siding while maintenance crews did special work up and down the right-of-way, returning at night to eat and sleep in the boxcars converted into living quarters. How I envied those forerunners of automobile trailer vagabonds! The minor daily maintenance of rock ballast, deteriorating crossties, and other such work was done by the section gang of four to six men and a foreman who rode back and forth on a handcar with counterbalanced up-and-down pump handles manually operated and connected with gearing for motive power. All the small boys in town envied this group, too, especially the foreman who rode in lordly idleness, doing no pumping nor tool work. My first childhood sweetheart's father became a section foreman after giving up his store on the east side of the tracks as unprofitable. The section gang used a lot of hardwood crossties, which the railroad bought from every farmer for miles around who had a patch of woodland and an adz. They were stacked in man-high pens on the unfenced east side of the right-of-way within the village limits, across from Mixon's store.

I may be wrong, but I think Grayson was the only station between Monroe and Alexandria, perhaps on the entire system, that had a husband-wife depot agent team. Mrs. Lizzie Mathis was the day agent; her husband John was on duty at night.

As was customary in those days, both were telegraphers for Western Union as well as the railroad, using a hand-operated sending key and the Morse Code. Orders from division points were dispatched on overhead wires to be relayed to train crewmen. It was a small drama of action when an engineer or fireman, depending on the direction of the train, leaned down from the cab and used one arm to hook a slender hoop with a handle holding the message as the train sped past, then dropped the hook before reaching the end of the cinder-paved platform.

The depot had three compartments: the waiting room at the south end for White Only (Colored waited on the platform); the agent's office in the center with a three-sided bay window for visibility up and down the track; and a freight room at the north end. There were manually operated levers on a shelf behind the center section of the window, and both Mr. and Mrs. Mathis had to pull and push these back and forth from time to time to operate the metal semaphore arms with red and green lights atop a tall pole across the track on the east side.

Every boy in town and the adults too, I suppose, knew that both arms sticking out horizontally meant that no trains could pass through pending clearance orders. Both lowered meant "All clear." The west arm down and the east one up mean trains going south had clearance, while those going in the opposite direction did not and had to go in the hole. The red and green lights that shone in keeping with the positions of the metal arms gave the "Stop" and "Go" signals at night.

My fascination with the railroad and its rolling stock did not extend to riding on the passenger trains. All my life I have disliked all conventional forms of transportation. I fly when I can now, not because I like it, but because the trips are over sooner. Passenger trains are not only as dull as planes, but aggravating. They imprison you interminably and tediously. They jiggle (or did when I last rode one) so badly you can't read as on a plane. Looking out through a window is like peering myopically at a scenic film with no pattern, running backward. The only thing possible to do is to sit and reflect, and for that I prefer a stationary seat in front of a log fire or a grassy spot under a tree.

But riding freight trains unlawfully was something else,

and it was one of the pastimes of young teeners in my time in Grayson; a practice frowned upon by most parents but tolerated by most indifferent crewmen. It was so much more satisfying than day coach travel to stand or sit on a swaying boxcar, smell coal smoke, feel the small sting of cinders, and look from side to side at two almost limitless panoramas unfolding just for you, even if the scenery wasn't very interesting.

The northbound freight trains had to chuff up a slight grade at Grayson, and their normal speed was just a bit faster than a boy could run. But there was a trick, easily mastered, by which it was possible to run alongside for a few paces on the depot's cinder platform, grasp the lowest rung of the side ladder and the iron stirrup depending below the car, and flip aboard in reasonable safety.

Once on the moving train, the ride stealer could select among such choice positions as the top of a boxcar, the narrow side walks of a tank car, the inside of an open and empty coal car with walls low enough to look over (a gondola), or a flatcar empty or loaded with stacks of pungent pine lumber.

The practice was to hop a freight and ride north about ten miles to Riverton, a water-tank stop for all trains, wait there for a southbound freight, and head back toward Grayson.

There was one hitch to this elastic round trip schedule. Southbound trains were going downgrade through Grayson and usually their speed was too great and dangerous to permit jumping off even when using a feet-first sliding technique in the gravel ballast. The alternative was to ride on south to Kelly, seven miles away, where the grade dipped both up and down. Here speeds were reduced in each direction so that it was possible to alight from one train and flip another later for the return trip. Then, back in Grayson, getting off was no problem on the upgrade.

It often was possible and time-passing if not exactly thrilling to spend a whole Saturday, Sunday, or a summer vacation weekday in this fashion.

For shorter and more certain trips there were the two daily merchandise delivery freight trains called Locals—one southbound around midmorning from Monroe, and the other northbound and scheduled to arrive at midafternoon from Alexandria. Both made all stops and met somewhere down the line below Grayson, depending upon how closely each stuck to its schedule. Thus, it was possible to make the round trip in a reasonable period of time. The flaw here was that the Locals also carried paying passengers seated on lengthwise leather benches inside the caboose. The crews were of no mind to let time-killing youths ride free elsewhere on the trains.

This taboo was enforced in my time by a chief brakeman, a heavy-handed and light-complexioned mulatto called Buck, who rode the southbound Local one day and the northbound the next. However, quite often there were a great many supplies from Monroe to be unloaded for Grayson's too numerous merchants, and if Buck was in a good mood or poor condition, he would permit two or three of us boys to help him and another brakeman carry sacks of flour, sugar, and the like from the side door of a boxcar across the platform to the freight room.

As a reward, we were permitted to ride south to the rendezvous with the northbound Local, where Buck passed the word to his opposite number. If Buck's mood happened to be especially good and the conductor busy in his caboose "office," we could sit on the benches with the paying passengers, most of them drummers making quick business calls on one or more merchants at each freight unloading stop. Most of the time, though, we were expected to ride the boxcars or other cars designated by Buck, and we really preferred it that way.

There were two methods of stealing rides on passenger trains, both a bit dangerous and definitely frowned upon by the railroad: riding the blinds and riding the rods.

The "first blinds" were just behind the coal tender, where there was a narrow platform facing a recessed space leading to an always locked door of the first baggage car. The "second blinds" were precarious perches on both sides of the closed passageways between coaches the entire length of the train.

The rods were parallel air brake and steam heat pipes running along lengthwise a foot or so below the coach floors and about the same height above the roadbed. The ride stealer either stretched in a spraddle on a couple of these pipes or on a plank laid across several of them. In either position, ballast rocks were likely to be sucked up at high speeds to pepper the face.

Crewmen of passenger trains kept a pretty close watch when they could, especially on the depot side at each stop, for riders of the blinds and the rods, and chased them. It was not easy to escape detection by night and almost impossible in daylight except when there was some sort of cover available for hiding while waiting on the side of the track opposite the depot.

Other boys in town dared this form of adventure, but I stopped it after a few times, because of Grandpa's special sense of what was permissible, if not good, and what was not to be condoned at all for moral reasons. (He managed somehow to keep abreast of what was going on in my crowd most of the time.)

"I don't like any of this forbidden train riding business you and the other young hellions in town are doing," he told me one day. "But there's no way of preventing a normal boy from risking life and limb for excitement short of locking him up, and I don't think that's the answer.

"But you must consider other things than the danger," he went on. "When you steal a ride on a freight train, you take nothing of value to anyone and deprive the railroad of no revenue. When you ride the Locals, I understand you pay your fare with unloading assistance. That's a form of barter and not dishonest, even if the practice is not covered by railroad regulations. But when you steal a ride on a passenger train, that's unmistakable theft, and you're cheating the railroad; those trains are operated for passenger traffic profit. So, if you're doing it, stop it, and if you're planning to do it, don't. I won't have it."

When Grandpa spoke in such terms, I obeyed. The only times I was really tempted were when I wanted to see a movie, and his edict increased the cost of such entertainment from a dime to at least twenty cents and sometimes thirty cents.

One of the frustrations of my youth was that I seldom saw a movie through to the end. Most of them remained forever unfinished stories to me, and I hated to pay doubly or trebly for half-told tales.

Grayson had no motion picture house. The sawmill town of Clarks two miles south was owned, body and sidewalks, by the Clarks Lumber Company. It paternally operated at cost for its workers a commissary, an ice plant, a library, and a movie theater. Outsiders were neither encouraged nor forbidden to use these facilities.

Picture nights in Clarks were Tuesdays and Saturdays. The easiest way to get to Clarks from Grayson was by train. For me it was the only way, unless I wanted to go on foot or the bare back of Old Black. (In later years, a few more fortunate friends with the use of a family car sometimes gave lifts, but that was in double-dating days.) The southbound evening train, if on time, arrived in Clarks ten or fifteen minutes before the start of the single five-reel picture program lasting an hour or so. The northbound evening train did not run so conveniently. The lumber company arranged its entertainment to suit the convenience of its townspeople; and the railroad, presumably, was not even aware that its schedule was such that the northbound was due in Clarks about ten or eleven minutes, or half a reel, before the end of the feature picture.

Railroad fare between Grayson and Clarks was ten cents; and since I was forbidden to steal a ride, which was possible usually for the return trip when it was dark enough to cover a sneak climb to the blinds, I had to dig up a total of thirty cents to cover transportation and admission each time I indulged a fondness for westerns.

Since such a sum was not easy to come by, I made no attempt to attend every movie program at Clarks or even to go once a week. But I never failed to scrounge the money for a William S. Hart picture, and I always hoped that on these occasions the southbound would be on time and the northbound late. Sometimes a two-reel comedy, usually a Mack Sennett, preceded the feature, but I didn't mind missing that if the southbound was late. It was the northbound and the end of the western that mattered.

It seemed to me that the damned northbound showed a perversity that couldn't have been without malicious design. It frequently ran fifteen minutes, thirty minutes, or even an hour late on Sundays, Mondays, Wednesdays, Thursdays and Fridays. Almost never did it run so much as a minute late on Tuesdays and Saturdays.

The picture house was about two hundred yards from the Clarks depot. I usually managed to get a seat near a window on the south, or station, side of the theater. From there, unless the piano accompaniment to gunfire and the clatter of hooves on the silent screen was too loud, I could hear the north-bound blow its — — · — and ———— signals a minute before it came to the stop at the station.

Thus warned and timing every movement, I could ease myself over the window sill, cling there for one last greedy glimpse of Bill Hart sheathing his smoking guns after finishing off half a dozen rustlers, and sprint across the back lots to the station, arriving just in time to swing aboard the front passenger coach as the train pulled out. It was no comfort to know that the picture would be just ending as I stepped from the train, having parted with my last dime to the conductor, at the Grayson depot.

Sometimes, if the action on the screen was too excruciatingly exciting and the outcome too doubtful, I would remain seated when the whistle blew, shut my ears to the puffing approach of the northbound, and watch the picture to the horse-ride-into-the-sunset end. The price of this indulgence was a half-hour walk home in the dark, a dreadful way to wind up an evening out.

There were two routes that could be followed on foot from Clarks to Grayson. One was the railroad track, where the crossties were laid exasperatingly too close together for comfortable stepping on each and too far apart for skipping.

The alternate choice, even less inviting, was to take to the road alongside the track. In those days, before it was straightened and paved, it meandered off at intervals into deep, dark woods. After an hour or so with Bill Hart it seemed only too likely that those shadowy trees and bushes sheltered dangerous outlaws; and though I fully intended to clean them out of there some day, I was not anxious to encounter them before I had acquired my two six-guns and a cow pony. . . . Rather than walk either forbidding route, I usually caught the north-bound and wondered how the story came out.

One well-remembered night I was crossed up twice. I dropped out of the window, responding reflexively to the whistling of a locomotive, and sped to the station platform only to discover that I had been betrayed by a special freight running ahead of the northbound, which was not due for nearly half an hour. I had seen only about half of the film.

I raced back to the theater and tried to convince the woman ticket taker that I had already paid my way in and had left the theater by mistake. She had seen no one leave; and she had foiled such artful dodgers before. I debated briefly with myself, then parted with the third and last dime of my evening's budget and saw the rest of the picture, this time missing about half a reel in the middle instead of the end.

Since I had no money for train fare and no intention of defying Grandpa's edict against riding the blinds, I didn't even listen for the whistle of the northbound.

When the show was over, I chose the railroad track for the dark walk home and—wouldn't you know it—I had to step off it on the outskirts of Clarks to let that perverse north-bound go by.

It was fifteen minutes late that night.

# IX

Louisiana, now one of the five so-called Deep South states, once was a territory that embraced most of the Mississippi River Basin. In 1724 Territorial Governor Bienville promulgated the *Code Noir* which not only set apart Negroes, free and in slavery, and governed their lives and places in society, but provided for the expulsion of Jews from the New Orleans colony under penalty of imprisonment and confiscation of property. This is said by the historians I studied in Louisiana to be the first government decree in this country to discriminate against both Negroes and Jews. It also set up Catholicism as a state religion more than six decades before the First Amendment established the policy of separation of religion and state. The historians reported these matters dispassionately, neither approvingly nor disapprovingly.

Thus Louisiana, which in my time had about half its present 3.5 million population, has a longer record than most states of discrimination against its minorities. The black population was something like 30 percent of the total but its density varied widely among the sixty-four parishes and the pattern of racial prejudice did not necessarily follow that of the population ratios. There were no Jews at all in Grayson and I never knew their prevalence elsewhere in the state, but in my early-century decades, Negroes were in the majority in seventeen parishes. These were mostly in the Delta from Iberville in the northeast corner to the Floridas and the Sugar Bowl. The hill country of my north-central section had been settled largely by descendants of Protestant Anglo-Saxon stock; and the percentage of Negroes in Caldwell Parish was much smaller than those of the state and the South as wholes, perhaps no greater than the nation's overall 10 percent. Yet, I grew up with white racism and shared it until I was taught better. Some instances of it were extreme.

One day during a round trip on the Locals under the tolerant aegis of the half-white brakeman Buck, I noticed for the first time a crude sign on the outskirts of a small community I will call "Notown." It warned:

> Don't Let The Sun
> Set On You
> In This Town
> Nigger

On that trip another boy and I were being allowed to sit in the caboose, since there were no paying passengers and the conductor was busy in his partitioned desk space. At the Notown stop Buck made no move to go to the depot platform and when we asked if our help would be needed there he replied with a look, not of hatred, but of utter contempt:

"Let the agent and the merchants unload their own damned stuff. I don't care if they never get it, and I hope it rots in the stores before anybody buys it, but if it is bought by any of the white trash here, I hope it gives them the miseries."

That evening I told Grandpa about the sign, without mentioning Buck's reaction, and asked what he thought of it. He replied promptly with a look that almost matched the brakeman's.

"No self-respecting person, white or black, would ever set foot in Notown by day or by night. It isn't a fit place to live, to visit, or to pass through without holding your nose. The people who live there are without humanity."

I could tell he was ready to express some strong opinions on this subject, so I prompted him by asking:

"What in the world would niggers do after sundown that caused somebody to put up that sign? What do they think would go on after dark if niggers were in town?"

"Don't use that word," he said automatically. "The Negroes probably wouldn't do anything except mind their own business as they usually do here and most places. But I know what the hypocritical white men do by day in Notown and what they would like to do by night, as their forebears have been doing for generations."

"What?"

"Practicing daytime bigotry and nighttime miscegenation," he snapped.

"What's that last word mean?" I asked, whipping out a notebook and pencil.

"I'll tell you how to spell it," he said, and did so. "You can look up the meaning when the time comes that you will understand it. If I raise you as I should and intend, you'll never practice it or any other form of adultery."

"I know what that means," I boasted.

"Some things can be learned too soon," he said enigmatically.

"Well, what's any of this got to do with that sign at Notown?"

"Well," he said, considering. "Perhaps I can tell you a few things for future reference.

"Too many white men in the South have been talking ever since I can remember about Negroes lusting after and raping their women. The truth is that it's the other way around; that's why you hardly ever see a Negro with a coal black skin nowadays. They don't get their light complexions from white mothers but from white fathers who forced themselves upon Negro women in most cases. In this country if a person has even a tiny Negroid strain in his blood he is classed as a Negro.

"In southern Louisiana they used to have for reference an actual percentage or fractions chart with graded names for all persons having mixed blood. You can look it up some time if you want the whole chart; it ranges from a griffe, who is 75 percent black with a Negro father and a mulatto mother, to an octoroon, 12.5 percent black and spawned by a white man and a quadroon woman. But they are all classifications of Negro.

"In New Orleans, even during my time in St. Helena Parish, quadroon females lived openly, but in separate quarters from wives, with highly regarded young men in Creole society.

"It was considered quite the thing," he recalled musingly, "and to tell the truth, I had more respect for those young bloods and their custom than for some plantation owners and the sneaky way they went about having Negro women for pleasure, betraying their wives.

"Most wives pretended they didn't know what was going on, but they couldn't help knowing that the master of the plantation often visited a certain cabin in the quarters of nights. Some men even went so far as to install a favorite female from the quarters in the big house in the guise of a sleep-in domestic, who never was required—as the other servants noticed of course—even to learn how to boil water or change a baby's diaper.

"In the little towns of the redlands, where there are no plantations or masters, the lecherous men, married or single, still visit what they call Niggertown at night, or meet the females somewhere else. Sometimes they pay them; sometimes they just take them; but occasionally, I understand, it's a mutually satisfactory arrangement. I've never had anything but criticism for adultery, but I could forgive miscegenation if it weren't for the masculine hypocrisy. . . . Oh, well, this is all over your head now—I hope. Go take in a couple more armloads of stove wood before supper."

True, his discourse was quite a bit beyond my complete comprehension, as were others at the times I heard them, only to sink in later; but there were other aspects besides sex of the relationship of the races that confused me.

I puzzled over my relationship with Buck the brakeman, for example. According to the handed-down beliefs accepted by me and my contemporaries, he was our inferior because he was a mulatto and therefore by definition a nigger—who just naturally couldn't be the equal of any pure white person, young or old. Yet . . . Buck held a position of authority in a part of my world and could grant or deny a coveted privilege as effectively and finally as any white adult. So, in our relationship, who was superior and who inferior? And I couldn't forget the look on his face and the attitude, as reflected by his words, toward the white folks of Notown whom he refused to serve because he despised them. Could it be that Buck really felt those white merchants and their customers were lower-class people than he and undeserving of his respect or even the services he was paid to give them? And—unthinkable! —could he be right?

There were not many Negroes in our community, and I knew very little about them. There was the usual squalid ghetto at the south end of the village called Niggertown by the whites, but I had never been there. It was my impression that it consisted of only a dozen or so shanties; a little un-painted frame church without even a steeple that served also as a schoolroom when there was schooling; and nothing else worth mentioning or remembering.

There was an ancient crone, almost a caricature mammy who actually wore a red bandana around her kinky white hair and smoked a foul-smelling clay or corncob pipe. She came up from Niggertown to help out for a couple of days at hog-killing time, and slept for one night wrapped in a blanket on the brick hearth in front of the fireplace in one of the two south bedrooms. She was regarded as a "Character," steeped in superstitions and with a mindful of old sayings and home remedies. She was called Aunt Liza, and nobody paid any attention to what she said, however scandalous or disrespectful it sounded through her chuckles, because of her age. Then, there was Wes, a black boy about my age and the son of a sharecropper on a small farm somewhere back of the Hendricks place. He sometimes helped around our place and we played together, amicably but always observing the social customs based upon the assumption (by me and perhaps by him, too) that he was inferior to me in all measurable qualities because he was black and I was white.

That was about the extent of my knowledge of Negroes. My interest in them wasn't great either, but I was put out, not by Grandpa Blackman's unorthodox attitude and outspoken comments to me and anyone else who would listen, but by one custom he followed. That was the lifting of *his* hat to Negroes who tipped *theirs* to him as a salute in passing.

That just wasn't done in Grayson, or anywhere else that I knew of, but Grandpa didn't care in the least who saw him doing this or what they thought of him.

Jeff Brannigan was a large black man who lived on a farm up the road a piece toward Columbia. It seemed to me to be our unhappy fate while driving to town on the slide always to meet Jeff, driving a matched pair of mules and a sturdy double wagon, on the way home.

As Jeff passed us, the wheels of his wagon almost scraping our vehicle in the narrow road, he would doff his old felt hat and say with a wide, slow smile, "Howdy, Mr. Blackman." My grandfather would lift his equally shapeless hat so high that the sunlight glinted on his untidy gray hair and say courteously, "Good morning, Jeff," or "Good evening, Jeff."

One day, after I had become acutely aware that no other white man in the community ever lifted his hat in response to a Negro's greeting—or to another white man's for that matter, unless the white man happened to be accompanied by a woman—I protested.

"Grandpa, why do you tip your hat to a nigger?"

"Why, son, he tips his hat to me. And don't use that word."

"I know, but that's what everybody else calls them. And he's got to tip his hat to you. You're a white man."

"Oh, no; he's just being polite because he feels that way, not because he thinks I expect it. And would you have a white man be less polite than a Negro?"

While I pondered the logic of that, thinking it might be an adequate retort the next time my grandfather's odd behavior was brought up tauntingly by my contemporaries, he laughed. "That's not original with me," he said. "Someone else—Lincoln, maybe—said it first and said it better."

But my embarrassment continued and it was even more acute when Jeff's wife, Sarah, sat on the spring seat beside him, dressed in her Sunday best for town.

Grandpa would lift his hat in response to Jeff's salute and say, "Good evening, Jeff. Good evening, Sarah." Sarah would bob her kinky head and look almost as fussed as I did.

"Grandpa!" I exclaimed after one of these occasions. "You shouldn't tip your hat to a nigger woman. It doesn't look right. It just isn't—" I stopped, unable to put into words my sense of society's mores being violated.

"Sarah is Jeff's wife," Grandpa said patiently, as though that explained everything.

"But she's a nigger woman!" I protested.

"She is Jeff's lady," he corrected me. "All things are relative, and don't you see that the more that is so, the more they are the same? As Jeff's wife, Sarah is entitled to as much respect from me as I demand from other men for your grandmother."

Grandpa was incorrigible and hopeless, I concluded sadly, but before I resigned myself to that fact completely, I wondered whether his eccentric conduct just might be an elaborate joke. Perhaps that was his way of teasing me, of mocking Jeff, and of shocking the community, which I knew he regarded most of the time with more amusement than esteem. Knowing him as I did by that time, this didn't seem very likely, but the next time he and Jeff went through their little ritual, I watched Grandpa closely. I could detect no hint of mockery, no secret amusement, in his steady blue eyes, no reservations whatever in his courteous greeting.

"Grandpa," I said reflectively as Jeff's wagon passed on down the road, "you act like you really think Jeff is as good as you, your equal. Why, you act like you really *respect* him."

"Son," he said slowly, "it may take a little time, but some day you will get your sense of values straightened out and you will see these things in their true light. I certainly *do* respect Jeff Brannigan. I have the deepest respect for him, and I'll tell you why. You see that team of mules he drives?"

That was another sore point with me. "He drives a lot better rig than that slide of ours," I said accusingly.

"Certainly. He needs a better rig. Jeff farms sixty acres of creek bottom land and he needs two mules. I've retired from commercial farming, and Old Black and the slide are all I need and more. Well, what I started to say was that I loaned Jeff the money to buy the first of those mules when he quit sharecropping and started out on his own farm."

"You did?" I said, aghast. "You loaned him money for that, but you wouldn't loan any to Mr. Wassell for the same thing, and he's a white man. I heard you tell him you didn't have any to spare, when everybody knows you have."

"I wouldn't lend Jim Wassell a nickel," my grandfather said judiciously, "unless he gave me a dime for security. He's not in Jeff's class. I loaned Jeff money to buy a mule without security, and within a year he not only paid me back when I didn't ask for it but he had saved enough money to buy a second mule for cash. I respect Jeff for that. I respect any man who works hard, treats his family well, and gets along with his neighbors. But those are material things. I admire him because he has managed to keep his dignity and his self-respect under conditions that would drive me out of my mind if I were in his shoes. All his life, he has had to put on a show of respect for trashy people he knows in his heart are not his equals, much less his superiors."

"I bet he hates to tip his hat to you," I said spitefully, knowing better. "I bet he only does it because you are a white man and he thinks he has to, like to all the others."

"Ah, there you do Jeff and me both an injustice. I have a good, comfortable feeling that when Jeff tips his hat to me he does it *in spite of* my being a white man." Grandpa smiled when he saw the startled look on my face.

"And furthermore," he said, ending the discussion, "I'll bet that if I turned black overnight, Jeff would be the last to notice it."

# X

Grandpa Blackman seemed to make an effort in all situations in his sphere of activities, involving not only human beings but animals, to imagine "how the other fellow feels about it," as he put it. He certainly had his moments of irascible reaction to provocation by people with whom he dealt in which the "other fellow" probably had good reason to feel that he was the victim of unkindness, but I don't believe Grandpa was capable of cruelty to man or beast. I recall one incident involving an animal and me that he noted as an illustration that injury or worse could be caused involuntarily through failure to put oneself in the "other fellow's" place.

One of my summer chores was fetching home a couple of cows from the Back Forty for the evening milking. To reach the entrance to this tract, part pasture and part woodland, I walked through a lane that separated a twenty-acre field and the Near Pasture of equal size. Rail fences bordering the pieces of land and forming the lane were embroidered with blackberry briars.

This rather pleasant walk was over a gentle rise that descended into a little grassy glade that was a sort of foyer to the wooded entrance to the Back Forty. A dim path wound through the trees and bushes to the meadow section, which had been an old cultivated field, now abandoned to grass. The cows usually were waiting for me with heavy udders at the end of the lane. If they were not, I had only to call "Soooo-o-o-o-o cow," and presently they would come plodding along the path, lowing gently with the discomfort of needing to be milked or suckled by their calves (both occurred in common farm practice at that time). I would open the bars and follow them home to the milking pen beside the big barn.

One evening, when I reached the beginning of the glade, I saw a rabbit sitting on its haunches in the grass a dozen feet from the bars. I reached for something to throw, a boy's instinctive reaction. My hand closed on a pine knot, about twice the size of a hand grenade and similarly shaped, which probably had fallen long before from a slide load of firewood.

I let fly with it, and the rabbit, untouched, leaped twice and vanished through the wire fence into the woods. I took the cows home and thought no more of the rabbit.

The next evening when I reached the glade the rabbit was sitting in the same spot. This time, the only missile I could find quickly was a clod of dirt, which disintegrated into dust before it had gone half way to the target. But the rabbit vanished again as before. After I had let the cows into the lane, I searched for the pine knot, found it, and dropped it at the spot where I had first picked it up—just in case.

The rabbit did not fail me the next evening, and only once did it ever not be there during the weeks that followed. It was always in the same place, give or take a couple of feet, and the moment I saw it, I scooped up the pine knot and threw it in what came to be one continuous motion. Then I retrieved the missile and left it where I could use it the next time.

Rabbits always run in zigzag fashion. One leap to the left and one to the right were just enough to take this one to the fence, through which he could scuttle to the screening safety of the underbrush. So, instead of throwing directly at the rabbit where he sat, I would lead him, as a hunter with a gun leads a bird on the wing, and aim at the spot where experience had taught me to expect him to be at the end of my throw, about twenty feet away. It was the motion of my arm that started him into action.

After a few days I learned by trial and error that my point of aim should be midway of the rabbit's second, or zag, leap. Thereafter, it was a matter of perfecting my aim. I got better and better, until at last a throw whizzed so close behind the rabbit that it caught him on the roll at the end of his leap, upsetting him in the grass. He thrashed around wildly for an instant, then regained his feet and resumed his flight, apparently uninjured.

The next day there was no rabbit there when I went for the cows. I was disappointed and a little hurt, like a swain stood up by his date, but most of all I felt apologetic. I lingered a few minutes, peering into the underbrush, wishing there were some way I could convey to the rabbit that I was sorry I had upset and scared him.

I arrived a bit early on the next trip. I hadn't much hope, but there he was, sitting motionless, as usual. I was so pleased that I yelled "Hello!" and the shout galvanized the little animal into action faster than lobbing the pine knot ever had. But he came back the next day and he continued to come back.

After that, I deliberately pulled my shots. My object was to see how close I could come to the rabbit without hitting him. My aim became very accurate, but the margin between safety and danger for the target was too narrow to permit anything less than perfect control.

That sort of perfection is something not even the most skilled of professional baseball pitchers ever achieve, and it was certainly beyond attainment by a small boy with a pine knot. . . . The inevitable happened.

One evening I scooped up the missile from a tuft of grass and threw it as usual with all the careless good will of a man saying hello in passing to a friend of long standing. But the moment it left my hand, I knew. I checked my follow-through abruptly and tried to close my eyes when the rabbit began his second leap, but I couldn't. The heavy pine knot caught him at the back of the head, between the long ears. He rolled over twice, kicked convulsively a few times, and lay still.

Each of those death kicks registered with sickening force in my stomach. Nauseated, I ran and picked up the soft, limp animal. I could hardly see through my tears. The rabbit was dead, of course. With a movement of instinctive revulsion, I threw him over the fence far into the underbrush.

My observant grandfather noticed the stains of unusual tears that evening and gently asked their cause. I told him about the rabbit, and in a dither of grief and guilt I cried:

"But it was only a game, Grandpa. I didn't mean to kill him, really I didn't. I didn't want to hurt him, even. It was just a game."

Grandpa nodded understandingly, then shook his head gravely, and I knew from experience he was going to do a bit of moralizing.

"I know how you felt," he said, "but your approach to what you call a game was unilateral. You didn't really try to imagine how the other fellow felt about it, and he couldn't tell you. To the rabbit, that glade was his domain, and you were an intruder who chased him into the woods each evening before he was ready to go.

"It might be a good idea," he concluded, "to bear in mind the next time you invent a game involving 'rabbits' of any kind, that it's only fair to consult the other fellow by trying to put yourself in his place. If you don't know and can't imagine how he feels about it, then it's not a game. It's a one-sided sport, like hunting birds and beasts with a gun, and the pleasure is all yours."

# XI

---

Whether he liked and respected his neighbors or not, Grandpa tried his best to get along with them. Sometimes, he went to what I thought were extremes to maintain amicable relations with persons he had to deal with or live near. His formal education (about which he was always vague; it probably ended with the fifth grade) did not include language, classical Greek word, *demos*, and one Latin phrase, *Vox populi, vox* or romance. But in his extensive reading he picked up one *Dei*. This he mispronounced and freely translated as "The voice of the people is the voice of God." I never quite came to share his faith in either, but years later when I read Carl Sandburg's paean to his fellow men ending "with a great bundle of grief the people march—the people, yes," I recalled that Grandpa had long ago before said very much the same thing in his own way.

"Most people are good at heart even in adversity, if you give them half an excuse to respond to good," he told me often. "And in the long run you can depend on people, in the singular or the plural, to be right, to do the proper thing, to reach the correct conclusions, to respond to their better instincts. Sometimes slow, but nearly always sure. *Vox populi, vox Dei.*"

He clung stubbornly to this conviction in the face of considerable evidence to the contrary. I recall one episode in particular that shook him but did not dismay him for long— in fact, his confidence was justified in the end, and he was not above gloating over it.

It had been his custom for as long as I could remember to go to his wooded section of the Back Forty on the first cool day of autumn to lay in a supply of firewood more than sufficient to last through the chilly but short winter. At first he had to use a hired hand to help him, but he dispensed with this paid labor as soon as I was old enough to pull one end of a crosscut saw without dragging on it.

One year when I was still a bit young for that sort of work, he had as a helper his son-in-law, Elias Grayson, who was in Grayson for a visit and said he needed the exercise.

Grandpa took me along that day to help clear away underbrush and do similar light auxiliary chores. He picked the trees and the two men sawed and split wood all day. When we paused at midday to eat some thick biscuit and meat sandwiches (midmorning coffee in a vacuum container that day), Uncle 'Lias wandered off into the woods and upon his return reported:

"I see Mr. Hackett likes this section of the woods, too, because there are signs over there that he has cut his own supply on his own side of the property line."

Mr. Hackett (not his real name) was the owner at that time of the adjacent wooded property on the south, with no fence between our land and his; there was no pasture acreage on it and none of the succeeding owners bothered to fence it in. Our cows seldom strayed when put to grass in the Back Forty.

Mr. Hackett was regarded as a rather sullen, bad-tempered, and generally disagreeable man. Grandpa looked thoughtful for a moment after the report by Uncle 'Lias of the close proximity of Mr. Hackett's woodcutting, but said nothing. He began to look worried though a little later when Neighbor Hackett rode up on his sorrell horse, looking secretly self-satisfied, and commented: "I see you're laying in a good supply." Without waiting for a reply, he rode on into the woods.

Grandpa's obvious forebodings proved sadly to be justified at the end of the day, after we had ricked up the last cord of a winter's supply of firewood ready for leisurely slide hauling home later. Mr. Hackett arrived on the scene with his horse-drawn wagon, and a son about my age named Eldon. Father and son, the latter looking a bit sheepish, began loading our wood into the Hackett wagon while we looked on in disbelief. Grandpa was the first to speak.

"Why?" he asked simply.

"My wood," Mr. Hackett said gruffly. "My trees. You're on my land. I just had it surveyed the other day." He pointed to a blaze on a tree just north of where we had been working.

"If you don't believe it," Mr. Hackett concluded defiantly, "have your own survey made."

Grandpa nodded. "I believe you, all right. But you knew this when you rode by here earlier today. It would have been more neighborly if you had told us then that the wood we were cutting would be legally yours. Even now, we can work it out; I'll give you an equal number of good trees on my side of the property line; you can cut them as you need them, and neither of us will be the loser."

"If you were fool enough to cut my trees without checking, that's your lookout," Mr. Hackett said sullenly. "It's my firewood under the law, and I'm taking it."

They continued loading. With high sideboards, the Hackett wagon held all the wood we had cut, an amount of wood that would have been a dozen of our slide loads. I watched outraged. Uncle 'Lias hefted his axe with obviously murderous thoughts. Even Grandpa looked pained, but maintained his calm demeanor. As the Hacketts drove away with our winter's supply of heating fuel, Grandpa shrugged his shoulders and said mildly:

"I guess he feels fate's against him, with an ailing wife and other troubles. I hear things haven't gone too well with him in some land and timber deals, and he probably has to take his misery out on somebody to get even. But I'll wager he's going to feel ashamed of this when he thinks it over."

"Oh, don't be so damned philosophical and—and—forgiving," Uncle 'Lias spluttered impatiently. "Hackett is just a mean cuss, that's all. He was born mean, and he'll stay that way all his life."

"Maybe not," Grandpa said. "You never can tell about people. Sometimes you think you have them figured out and then they fool you."

Uncle 'Lias snorted, but he rallied around to help again the next morning. He couldn't spare another full day. We went back to the woods and cut as much as we could in half a day, making sure this time we were on my grandfather's land. He and I began hauling it the next day. It wasn't enough to last the winter, and Grandpa meant to hire a hand and finish the job, but first one thing and then another prevented it.

The events that followed the timber poaching episode unfolded like a rural Greek drama with retributive overtones. Neighbor Hackett, his already ailing wife, and son Eldon all came down at once with influenza just before Christmas. When we got the news, Grandpa looked at me and I knew what was coming: he was going to enact his good-for-evil role, but knowing how I felt he was somewhat apologetic about it.

"It's up to us," he said. "Womenfolks in the town will do the nursing, but you're the logical one to go over and do the chores. We're the closest neighbors, and you know what has to be done. And, remember, it isn't just for him. Mrs. Hackett is a kindly soul and her lot has been a poor one."

So for a week, with reluctance and resignation, I went over to the Hackett place each morning and evening to feed the horse and chickens, draw the well water, and perform other tasks that had to be done around a farmhouse. Bitterest pill of all, I carried in armloads of firewood. I made a point of selecting "our" cutting because it was a bit too long for the Hackett fireplaces and had to be piled in slantwise. I hoped this would be noticed and serve as a reminder that Mr. Hackett had no real need to confiscate our ricks, since he had an adequate supply that he had cut to a length suitable for his andirons. . . . Mrs. Hackett was voluble in her expressions of appreciation for what I did, but Mr. Hackett and Eldon said nothing. Perhaps they were too sick. My feelings about their recovery were ambivalent, but they did get well and my volunteer service ended.

The denouement of this little drama was one I never would have dared to use in writing fiction because it was just too pat for verisimilitude.

Our half day of firewood cutting, never supplemented, was inadequate for the winter from the start, and a severe sleet storm after Christmas depleted our supply entirely. Grandpa faced the necessity of *buying* firewood, an unacceptable outlay for a farmer with a woodlot and little cash. But the weather prevented woodcutting, and Grandpa began asking around with intent to buy.

The plot pointing to the climax was as creaky as the wagon sounds Grandpa and I both heard in the middle of a frosty night after the incredible word got out that Old Man Blackman had been trapped into buying firewood. But he pretended surprise the next morning at the sight of the pile of firewood —almost all of our confiscated one day's production weeks earlier—neatly stacked in our side yard.

"You see," Grandpa crowed, his eyes gleaming with satisfaction, "I've always said people are really good at heart, and will respond to goodness, if you give them half an excuse. We gave Neighbor Hackett a whole excuse."

We both felt warm all the rest of that winter, but for different reasons, mine physical and his metaphysical.

# XII

———————

The amity between Grandpa and Neighbor Hackett continued for some time, but eventually it was strained by another incident. This involved Old Black and put Grandpa in a bind between a strong loyalty and a cardinal principle.

Grandpa doted on the old horse, and Grandma in one of her wryly sarcastic moods professed to see a definite resem-
of the same age, relatively, according to average human and
blance between them. She cited the facts that they were
equine life spans; both were stubborn, a bit eccentric, crea-

tures of habit—and understood each other better than brothers.

The delicate situation involving Grandpa, Mr. Hackett, and the villain of the piece—Old Black—was presaged by the appearance in our cow lot at milking time of a bobtailed calf. My grandparents were both puzzled by this peculiar deformity, but I thought I knew how the poor little beast had lost its tail brush, and it wasn't a pretty story.

Each day until the evening milking, the cows were put out to graze in the Back Forty's meadow, as I have related. The calves of mother cows that happened to be "fresh" at the time were kept in the Near Pasture. Old Black, when he was not being used, also was given the run of this tract as well as back lots, the lawn, or any other enclosure that enticed him. One day I saw him chasing a calf across the Near Pasture, which he was favoring at the time because the grass was greener.

A running calf hoists its tail like a fox's brush, and as Old Black closed in on the fleeing animal he stretched his neck, turned his head sideways and nipped at the waving tail as though he were biting off a stalk of green corn.

His bared teeth, at that distance, gave an appearance, not of ferocity, but of laughter. After the one nip, Old Black gave up the sport and began lazily munching grass. The calf skittered off to the far corner of the pasture, its tail still waving. I examined it that evening and found teeth marks, but they didn't appear to be serious. Apparently, however, Old Black kept at it on other occasions until he severed the brushy part of the tail.

I had had reason to suspect before that our saddle-slide-plow horse had once been a cow pony and had acquired a lasting dislike of cattle. I used him one day to round up our cows in the Back Forty when we had three of them, one a frisky young one with her first calf. She suddenly broke away from the others and ran in the opposite direction.

Before I knew what was happening, Old Black had wheeled after her like a vengeful demon. The cow swerved, and Old Black made a right-angle turn to head her off. He turned, but the worn-out old saddle and I did not. We sailed through the air in the same direction, landing in a heap on the meadow grass.

I wasn't hurt, and I looked up in time to see Old Black, like a sheepdog trained to work alone with a flock, shunting the maverick back to the other two, savagely snapping at her tail with his teeth. He then waited patiently for me to replace the useless saddle—the girth was broken—and I led him home, driving the cows ahead.

Grandpa knew nothing of Old Black's history, having bought him for fifty dollars from an itinerant horse trader passing through Grayson. He was called Black because of his color and because our name was Blackman. As the years passed, he was referred to as *Old* Black; and his coat turned a darkish rusty color at about the same rate that Grandpa's wedding coat, worn on special occasions, took on a greenish patina.

Whatever his background, Old Black worked well enough at the plow and at pulling the slide. Grandpa rode him quite often until the old saddle wore out entirely. He refused to buy another. Thereafter, only I rode the old horse, bareback except for a gunny sack to protect my pants from shedding hairs and sweat.

I discovered by accident that he had a saddle gait, which Grandpa identified as fox foot. It was easy riding, compared to his usual lumbering trot or gallop, but Old Black was a stubborn beast, and he seldom responded to the pinch at the back of his mane that was the signal to shift to the smooth gait. We got along fine though, because we also understood each other.

Although Grandpa knew Old Black's foibles, he was unwilling to admit to some of his knowledge. For his part, the wily old horse's understanding of his master was so thorough that he often took advantage of him and seemed to enjoy exasperating him. After school, during the spring plowing, I would go to the twenty-acre cornfield adjoining the Near Pasture (with the lane between) and relieve Grandpa at the plow for a couple of hours. Long before I reached them, I could hear Grandpa shouting, "Get up, there! Get along, you lazy old devil." He would flick him frequently across the rump with the free ends of the plow lines in a futile effort to enforce his commands. Old Black never paid the slightest attention to him; he continued at a pace so slow that at a distance I had to take a sighting on a fence post or bush to see any motion at all. The beast's ears signaled his attitude; they dropped like turnip leaves wilting under a summer sun.

"Laziest old horse that ever lived," Grandpa would grumble as I took over. "Oh well, see what you can get out of him before supper time."

The truth was that Grandpa was getting along in years, but wasn't ready to admit it, and Old Black's pace suited him just fine. I knew I was indulging in fantasy, but I liked to think that the old horse knew this and therefore ignored his master's furious pretense that he wanted more speed.

It was a different matter when I took hold of the plow handles and lines. I merely said, "Now get along, Old Black," and he began to move briskly at a steady pace that at least kept the plow biting into the soil without wobbling. His upthrust ears signified his understanding of the changed situation. Grandpa pretended never to notice this acceleration of speed as he set off to make the three o'clock coffee (which I would take a fifteen-minute recess for at the proper time). He also ignored the obvious fact that I had managed to cover more ground in two hours than he had all day up to the time I took charge.

I had a grudging fondness for the ornery, clever old nag, and I didn't want to get him into trouble by reporting his calf-chasing divertissement. When, however, a week or so later, a second calf appeared in the cow lot minus the effective fly-brushing portion of its tail, I decided it was unfair to defenseless creatures to keep silent any longer. I told Grandpa what I had seen and suspected.

"Well, what do you know about that!" he exclaimed. "Hitch the lazy old devil to a plow, and he acts like he's falling dead on his feet from age and overwork. Turn him loose in a pasture, and he chases little calves and bites off their tails. . . . Well, I'll fix him."

But when it came to a practical solution, Grandpa favored Old Black. He couldn't keep the horse locked in a stable all the time he wasn't being worked and he needed the grazing acreage of the Near Pasture. The calves, being too young to eat grass, were kept in the cow lot thereafter, and Old Black continued to run free in his usual leisure haunts; he was barred only from the cow lot.

This worked out all right until the day my grandmother greeted Grandpa at three o'clock coffee with some bad news:

"Mr. Hackett came by, buzzing like a hornet. Old Black has been jumping back and forth over that south fence into the other pasture Mr. Hackett bought some time ago from the Grayson property, and he has been chasing and biting his calves. None of them has lost a tail yet, but he says they get so upset they don't suckle as they should, and the cows aren't giving the same amount of milk. Sounds like a little far-fetched result of tail biting, but he's mad."

Those adjoining pastures, exactly the same size, had been for some time the subject of tentative negotiations between

Grandpa and Mr. Hackett. It was my understanding that Mr. Hackett wanted to buy our twenty acres and convert the two strips into one forty-acre pasture, since his property next to our Back Forty included no grazing land as ours did. Faced with Old Black's fence-jumping invasion of his neighbor's pasture, Grandpa gave no thought to buying or selling as a solution, but reached a sterner and what was for him a sad decision.

"Can't have more trouble with a good neighbor," he said, "and Mr. Hackett is trying now to be that, for all of his stubbornness. Can't keep Old Black locked up, so I'll just have to get rid of him, the calf-chasing old fool."

He proceeded promptly and sternly to do so. There was no ready local market, alas, for Old Black, because of his age and because word of his peculiar penchant for calf tail biting already had got around. But he persuaded a man named Abe Hawkins, a small-time farmer in a creek bottom off the high road to Columbia, to take the horse on a thirty-day trial basis, revocable by either party. Mr. Hawkins had a mule for plowing, but he needed—or said he wanted—another critter for utility work. And he had no cattle, as Grandpa learned by cautious inquiry. The thirty-day clause, I thought, must have been to give him time to think of some other solution to the Old Black problem, if there could be one. The price agreed upon was nominal.

As it turned out, Mr. Hawkins seldom used Old Black for any purpose except driving to town in his wagon on Saturdays. The way led past our place, and Grandpa just happened to be out front when Old Black went by on the first trip. I saw him first and noticed that he was moving along at a fairly brisk pace until he got a glimpse of Grandpa standing on the lawn a moment before Grandpa saw him. He promptly slowed down to the snail's pace that was his usual speed when

Grandpa was plowing or driving him. His new conditional owner's shouts and whip cracking had no effect on him whatever.

"Look at him!" Grandpa fumed as though this were something unusual. "What in the world is the matter with him? What do you suppose Abe Hawkins is doing to him? He must be starving him to death. He looks like he was on the way to the bone yard and would never live to get there."

"He looks and behaves the way he always did when you were handling him," I said impatiently.

Grandpa ignored this, but he refused thereafter to watch as Old Black went past, after learning the Saturday town visiting schedule of Mr. Hawkins. And on these subsequent occasions, the knowing old horse stepped along as briskly as though I had been at the reins; I chose to believe this was due solely to the fact that Grandpa was not in sight.

But Grandpa continued to wonder and to fret, and he stepped up negotiations with Mr. Hackett on a deal involving their adjoining pastures, to what end I didn't know. But after one of their sessions, from which Grandpa emerged irritated, I asked:

"If you don't want to sell, why don't you tell him so flatly and end the matter?"

Grandpa snorted. "He doesn't really want to buy. He just doesn't need a forty-acre pasture for one horse and two cows, and I think he'd like to get rid of them, too. He wants to sell, and he knows that when it comes to land, I'd rather buy than sell if I have a choice and the money. He keeps offering me ten dollars an acre for my twenty, so that when he gets around to saying, 'Well, buy or sell, either way,' he can nick me for ten dollars an acre. He knows I hate to sell land except to buy more somewhere else. Any land, if you treat it right, will never be worth less any year then it was the year you bought it. Best investment in the world, and it's more real than money or stocks or any symbol. Gives you a feeling of belonging to this earth and a part of it belonging to you—"

"Suppose," I said, interrupting one of his favorite discourses, "just suppose that Mr. Hackett really does want to buy and you were willing to sell. What would you ask for your twenty?"

"I bought all the land I own in Grayson for five dollars an acre," he said, "and I wish I'd had the cash on hand to pick up that next door twenty-acre pasture from Wiley Grayson at the same price when I had the chance. If I *had* to sell today, I wouldn't take a cent less than fifteen dollars an acre, but—"

He stopped and peered at me suspiciously, but I was looking as guileless as Old Black refusing to take a bridle bit.

"Seems to me," I said musingly, as though I were groping through a complicated financial deal, "that if you want fifteen dollars an acre for *your* land, you should be willing to pay the ten dollars you think Mr. Hackett wants for *his*." I added as a sort of afterthought: "You think he wants to sell and get rid of his livestock. It's too bad you don't own that twenty next door, because if you did, you could remove the fence, and Old Black wouldn't have somebody else's pasture to jump into and bite off the tails of innocent calves. And you've got the two hundred dollars cash now, because I heard you say the other day that somebody had insisted on repaying a loan for more than that amount, and you haven't had time to lend it to anyone else."

Grandpa chewed reflectively on a splinter. "You better go get in some stove wood," he said gruffly, and set off in the direction of the Hackett place.

I let the wood chore go. I knew the box in the kitchen was already full; that was the task Grandpa always came up with when he couldn't think of anything else for me to do. Instead, I departed for the Abe Hawkins farm to revoke in Grandpa's name a tentative horse deal before the trial period ended. I expected no hitch, and there was none.

Old Black was back in the old stable he sometimes had occupied by the time Grandpa returned with a signed agreement with Mr. Hackett to buy from him twenty acres of pasture land at ten dollars an acre, payable in cash upon transfer of title.

"He's in his stall and looking fine," I said without further explanation.

Grandpa favored me with a smile that I interpreted as sheepish, as to himself, and approving, as to me. "You'll do, Son," he said, and went off to the barn lot.

I followed a bit later and found him half poking and half stroking Old Black, who had slumped sleepily in the stall, his ears curling down, paying no mind at all to Grandpa, who was grumbling:

"Nothing the matter with you now, you old fool. All you need is a good workout tomorrow, and you're going to get it, if I live to face the dawn."

Then Old Black saw me and automatically straightened up and thrust his ears forward.

"Look at him!" Grandpa exclaimed. "The lazy old devil knows what I'm talking about."

Old Black quickly recovered from his reaction to my sudden appearance. He drooped again and his ears dropped to half-mast. I fancied the effect was that of giving me a knowing wink. I liked to imagine that he knew well he was back home to stay and that life again would be as it always had been on the Blackman farm.

# XIII

Old Black received recognition from an unexpected quarter and advanced my practical education a stage or two when the carnival came to Grayson one year during the week before school opened. From the point of view of both the show people and the residents, that was the best time for its appearance. Most of the crops had been harvested and there was more cash in circulation than at any other time of the year.

Unhappily, this relative prosperity did not apply to me; I was short of funds, as usual. Thus, I was alert for opportunity when I went to the grassy area just east of the school's agricultural buildings to watch the carnival set up for its week's stand. Opportunity came quickly. I was standing nearby when a flashily dressed man directing the erection of the merry-go-round bleated to an assistant:

"The blasted well picks this time to go dry. Look at the damned thing!"

He pointed to the offending well on the adjacent school property. A pipe had been laid from it across a fence to an open cylindrical tank near the merry-go-round. A man was pumping the handle furiously but only a miserable trickle of water came from the end of the pipe emptying into the tank.

"We couldn't get enough water there to operate a water pistol, let alone the engine for the merry," the self-important man was complaining. "We got no merry, we got no calliope. No calliope, no come-on for the carny."

He turned around and looked at me. "Where's the nearest water—pond, stream, anything?"

I pointed across the open field to the east. "There's a creek off there, about a quarter of a mile. It isn't running now, but the old swimming hole still has water in it."

"How the hell am I going to get it up here?" he asked nobody in particular. "I sure can't take the merry-go-round down to the crick." (Only Northerners call a creek a crick.)

"I have the use of a horse," I offered. "And a slide," I added.

"What's a slide?"

"It's a—it's just a slide. A thing on runners. You hitch a horse to it. If you can get a barrel, I could put it on the slide and haul water up from the creek and fill the tank and keep it filled, if the engine doesn't use it up too fast."

"Sonny boy," he said, "maybe we can make a deal."

We made a deal. The tank held four barrels of water, and

I filled it in four trips with Old Black hitched to the slide. My carnival employer, a Mr. Bascom, estimated—accurately as it turned out—that the engine would consume about one barrel of water in each hour of operation. Since the carnival was open from noon until ten o'clock at night, that meant ten round trips to the creek each day.

My pay, which I considered munificent at first, consisted of four five-cent tickets to the merry-go-round for each trip. In my figuring, that added up to twenty cents an hour, two dollars a day—a truly splendid remuneration for that time and my age. Actually, of course, the deal would cost the carnival nothing and put nothing tangible in my pocket, either. But I was eminently satisfied at the start with the arrangement. I had never had enough of riding a merry-go-round, and now I could get my fill of it. There was always time between hauling trips for a ride or two and I had the last hour of the night performances in which to use up my accumulated tickets. A dizzying prospect, in two senses of the word.

Grandpa had no urgent use for Old Black's services that week and no objection to my enterprise, except that he thought 10 P.M. was an unholy late hour for a boy—or anyone for that matter—to be awake and away from home. He shook his head in wonderment at my appetite for merry-go-round riding. But he conceded I had the right to enjoy myself in any way I liked that didn't bother anyone else.

"Those carnival people are a different kind of folks from us," he remarked. "It's good to get to know all kinds. You might even learn something from them, and you're old enough now to decide whether it's worth knowing and remembering. If not, it's always easier to forget things than to learn them."

After the first day, I was permitted to hop on and off the merry-go-round while it was in motion, as the ticket taker did, and that made the riding more exciting. I became expert at it. I would seize one of the upright rods with my right hand and cup my left over the knee of one of the nongalloping wooden horses, and thus flip myself aboard in a movement similar to that of swinging onto a passing freight train. I was the envy of the other young yokels visiting the carnival.

The ticket taker, who was tolerantly amused by me after he concluded I wasn't likely to get hurt or cause him trouble, seldom bothered after the first day to collect my pasteboard unless I happened to be in his path when he started his regular round during each ride. Thus, I soon was able to impress my pals by parceling out tickets and saying, "Go take yourself and your girl for a ride on the merry-go-round."

When my own girl of the moment showed up early in the second evening, I gave her several tickets, intending to join her for a couple of rides after my next trip to the water hole. But when I got back, she apparently had had enough of that ride. I learned that the fickle lass had been lured away by my pal Brownie, who had enough cash to satisfy her craving for a wider variety of carnival amusements.

The fascination of the carrousel had begun to pall for me, too; I began to feel discontented with my deal and to wonder how I could earn some cash to pay my way and my girl's to the rest of the attractions on the last night of the carnival. I had made a date already, having figured that with a full tank I could knock off hauling for the last three hours at least.

A friendly carnival booth attendant named Tony Burch solved the problem for me. Tony was a hunchback, about four and a half feet tall, who operated one of the so-called games of skill offering cheap prizes for almost impossible feats. He was less interested in me than in Old Black. I soon learned that Tony was crazy about horses, all kinds of horses, and why he didn't get a job in some racing stable I don't know. He even liked the wooden nags on the nearby merry-go-round and was the only one of the carnival folks ever seen on it. Now and then he would wander over from his booth when I arrived with a barrel of water to pat and rub down the droopy old horse hitched to the slide.

"That horse you got there," he told me, "used to be a fine quarter horse, I'll bet."

"He's pretty lazy," I said, not knowing exactly what a quarter horse might be.

"He's just old, that's all," Tony said. "He's all of seventeen years old, and horses hardly ever live past twenty or twenty-five. Where'd you get him? He came from Texas, I'll bet."

"I think so," I agreed. "My grandfather bought him from a man passing through who may have come from Texas, and I think Old Black used to be a cow pony."

"Of course," Tony said, "and the chances are that if he was treated right by his owner he won many a quarter race and side bets on Saturday afternoons and Sundays."

I didn't quite comprehend all this, but I liked the way he talked about Old Black; and it was my aim to treat my horse right too in appreciation for his work for me. Thus, when he indicated after the first trip on the fourth day of the carnival that he was thirsty, I let him drink from the barrel before emptying it into the tank.

"What the hell is this?"

I turned around in surprise and saw Mr. Bascom glowering at me.

"I pay you to haul water for my tank," he growled, "and you let your horse drink it. What kind of a deal is that? Let him drink from the crick."

"I'll make it up," I said mildly. "He was thirsty, and I didn't want to make him wait. You won't run out of water, I promise you."

"I pay you four tickets a barrel," he said irritably, "and I don't get a full barrel. So I'm docking you one ticket for this trip."

And he did just that. He tore off three perforated segments of pasteboard tape from his roll instead of the usual four, handed them to me, and stalked off to cope with whatever other problem it was that must have been the real cause of his ill temper.

Tony Burch, who had lounged up unobserved on Old Black's off side, now came around and glared balefully at Mr. Bascom's retreating back.

"Why, that cheap son of a bitch!" he snorted. "Charging a thirsty old horse for a drink of water. I hope he cries for water in a Methodist hell some day." (Tony had mentioned to me that he was a Catholic and complained there was no chapel in Grayson for Mass.) He turned to me now. "He's been playing you for a sucker, kid. I bet he never told you them pasteboards he gives you are good for any ride in the carny."

"What! No, he never did."

"That's the kind of cheapskate he is," Tony said scornfully. "He doesn't own just this ride, he owns the whole works, and the tickets are all the same, good for any ride on the grounds. But there's always room on the merry, and sometimes there ain't on the others. So he pays you off in wooden horses, when you could be taking your girl or your pals all around the layout."

By that time my anger was beginning to match Tony's, but in all fairness I felt obliged to point out that the merry-go-round alone had figured in our agreement and I was a willing party to it.

"Well, you didn't sign a contract," Tony snapped. "Make a new agreement. Tell the old horse hater that he'll have to fork up some cash from now on, or get another boy. He'll come across, because he knows he couldn't get anybody else to do what you're doing for four times as much—in cash."

I followed Tony's advice. On the next trip I grimly informed Mr. Bascom that he could make other water hauling arrangements unless he was willing to pay me thereafter half in cash and half in tickets. He exploded, accused me of welshing, and finally asked suspiciously:

"Who put you up to this?"

"My horse," I replied impudently. "He doesn't like you."

Mr. Bascom finally capitulated, as Tony had known he would, and thereafter I collected on each trip ten cents in cash and two tickets—good for any ride in the carnival.

On closing night, after I had staked out Old Black for a well-earned rest, my girl and I made all the rides and then, with my cash, tried our luck at the games.

Never did any yokel have such phenomenal luck! The explanation finally dawned on me as we made our last stop at Tony's stand, because I wanted to say good-bye, and my girl won a Kewpie doll with her first throw of a hoop to add to her collection of prizes. Tony winked at me.

"You can't lose unless we want you to lose," he said from the side of his mouth, "and you can't win if we don't want you to win."

Tony had passed the word around to his fellow operators, and they had cooperated. The game devices were fixed for control without detection and, after all, the cheap merchandise was not theirs. It was Mr. Bascom's, and so was the profit.

As we left the grounds, groggy from rides and laden with loot, Tony waved cheerily.

"Take care of that old quarter horse," he said, "and don't

take any wooden nickels after this for rides on wooden horses."

That was the first time I had ever heard any version of that old parting cliché about not taking any wooden nickels. I thought Tony's advice was real sound.

# XIV

---

Worm bait fishing was not a favorite outdoor sport with the boys of Grayson, and none of us had ever seen fly casting with rod and reel. Our thing was fish gigging in the Ouachita River and the ponds and sloughs of the bottom lands. This was a nocturnal sport and yielded a hundred mosquito stings for every finny catch.

The tools for fish gigging were a bright light and a barbed metal trident affixed to one end of a broom or hoe handle. The gig could be bought for a dime and it was no trouble to attach it to the pole. Ideally, a powerful spotlight should have been used, but we didn't know where to obtain one and couldn't have paid for it anyway. As a substitute, we filled a wire basket with oily waste, attached it to swing from the end of another five-foot pole and touched a match to it. The finest waste in the world for this purpose, we learned, could be obtained from the lid-covered metal boxes at each end of freight car axles. Coarse strands of heavy cotton twine were soaked in oil and stuffed into the boxes to reduce friction when the car wheels turned on the steel axle. The oil dried in time and if not replenished friction would set fire to the waste and the train would be halted until the brakemen put out the fire and packed in a new supply of stuffing. Railroaders called this a hot box. . . . We were considerate enough to steal only a small handful from any one box so as not to increase the potentiality of fire.

The technique of gigging for fish required a team of at least two, one to carry the light and the other to wield the harpoon. There could be more than one harpooner. Walking along the water's edge, the boy in front would hold the flaming waste out from the bank. The bright light would blind the fish, usually perch or crappie, as they slept nosed in toward the bank a few inches below the surface, usually resting their bellies on the bottom. The gigger would hold his weapon poised above the fish for a moment, allowing for the distortion of true position caused by refracted light, and then plunge the three barbed prongs into the scaly back. The catch would be lifted out wildly flopping and dropped into a bucket serving as a creel.

The expedition would end when the supply of oil waste was burned away.

Our gigging was for fun, not for food. With one exception, fish was not a favorite viand in my time and community. The finny morsel that appealed to all appetites was the lowly fresh-water catfish, called mud cat by fishermen and *Opladelus olivaris* by scientists. Uninitiated Northerners class catfish with possum and chitlings, strictly "soul" food. As a matter of fact, Negroes and underprivileged po' white trash in the South had this delicacy to themselves until those connoisseurs of food, the traveling drummers, got wise to a good thing. Finally, the landed gentry, what was left of them, were converted and eventually in many parts of the South catfish farms were cultivated commercially to meet the demand.

There was always one public eating place in the river towns that specialized in catfish and hush puppies, sometimes with turnip greens; these drew patronage from miles around. The drummers would detour half a day out of their way to feast on catfish at such meccas as Catahoula Court. This was in Jonesville, in or near which several of my aunts and uncles lived. An older, generous cousin named Lamar Adams took me there once when we were both visiting Aunt Effie and Uncle Ernest in nearby Utility.

Eating a meal in a restaurant was a great and rare treat for me. There was none in Grayson—boarding houses, yes, but no restaurant—and I seldom enjoyed café cooking except when I went to Monroe or to visit relatives in Catahoula Parish.

The area around Jonesville was ideal catfish country. Within one mile the Ouachita becomes the Black and into it empties the Tensas and Little Rivers. Thirty miles south the Black flows into the Red (without noticeably changing its color) and after another thirty miles becomes the hard-to-spell-and-say Atchafalaya. This runs roughly parallel to the Mississippi and empties into the Gulf of Mexico some distance west of the three mouths of the Father of Waters.

Catfish abounded in all these streams and commercial fisher-men caught them on trotlines to supply public eating places and home cooks.

Catahoula Court, on the edge of town, was like thousands of roadside restaurants all over the nation before the chains proliferated. There was a row of booths down the side of one wall, flanking several evenly spaced tables between two en-trances. It was nearly 2 P.M. when we went in and the place was almost deserted. We sat in a booth.

"Catfish for two," Lamar told the waitress. "If we aren't too late for dinner."

"Never too late for catfish," the woman said cheerfully. "Anything on the side?"

"Not a thing, thank you," Lamar said.

There was a reasonable wait during which I could envision the scaleless fish rolled in meal—any meal available although real sticklers insisted upon fresh stone-ground corn—sinking into a pot of deep, gently seething fat oil, head, whiskers and all, and turning a sandy-brown color.

The fish came, each on an oblong platter with a clutch of french fried potatoes scattered over the head and the visible side of the body scored with the chef's knife before frying to make easier the forking. The salad contained the outer green leaves of lettuce instead of those tasteless, plastic composition, pale layers of something later called for unfathomable reasons iceberg.

The pure white flesh of the fish was flaky, tender as curd yet not dry—oh, there's no describing the taste of catfish to anyone who has never savored and compared a wild musca-dine with a domestic grape, for example. There is no sim-ilarity in the experiences, of course, but that is the sort of distinction there is between catfish and rainbow trout, to name just one familiar Northern delicacy.

We silently cleaned off one side, finding no small bones to shun or spit out surreptitiously, and turned over the carcass to polish off the scored other half. We drank only water with the meal; I learned long afterward that rosé wine complements catfish nicely, or if no such potable is available, green tea goes well with it.

Our splendid repast cost Lamar fifty cents for each of us, a whole dollar for a meal for two. For anything other than catfish, we would have considered that an outrageous price.

Lamar left nothing for the waitress—tipping in that part of the South was unheard of then—but he sent back a dime for the chef. We knew from experience that he would be a very black, slightly sweaty Negro in a wilted white cap and soiled but somehow still fresh apron.

We also could guess what he would do with the *pourboire*. As soon as he got off work he would forget such prosaic fodder as catfish and go to a chili parlor in his own neighborhood to squander the entire dime on a bowl and a beer.

# XV

Mention of the carnival near the school grounds reminds me that I have been remiss in reporting on school in Grayson— which was what brought us there from Manifest. I spent all of my elementary and high school years in the consolidated school that had been nearing completion when we moved to the village.

I did not realize then that I was a traitor to my age group —mythical, typical American boys who are supposed to hate school and rejoice when the summer vacation begins. I didn't hate it at all; I loved to go to school. I was unhappy when school let out each May for the long summer and I yearned for classes to begin in the fall.

This is not to suggest that I was an exceptional student or even that I learned very much in school. I think that whatever education I have was obtained in spite of teachers, curricula, textbooks, and homework. These things started mental gymnastics and exploratory reading, and I suppose I became as nearly self-educated as Grandpa Blackman.

Oh, I attended all classes dutifully; I studied, did my homework, and made good grades; but I *learned* only the things that interested me. The rest I merely memorized as quickly as possible and remembered only long enough to meet my immediate requirements and carry out the assignments of the teachers. Each year, as soon as I got the approved textbooks I read them through as fast as I could, and looked at them thereafter only as guides in the recitations and paperwork required for each day, month, and term of the school year, for grading purposes.

I liked school in spite of schoolwork. It had people, lots of people: a teacher for each of the eleven grades (a twelfth has since been added) plus one for agriculture and one for domestic science; and an enrollment greater than the population, since boys and girls came each day from homes miles away in the country in covered horse-drawn vehicles called wagonettes.

Individuals differ from one another but their own personalities also vary and it was fascinating to watch them change from day to day, from year to year, from mood to mood, from circumstance to circumstance. I've never encountered a human being, even a foolish or evil one, who did not have at least one facet to his character worth discovering and studying. So it was that in school seeing everyone again each fall and for eight months thereafter was wonderful; saying goodbye to them each spring was saddening.

I found the then seven grades of elementary school and the subjects taught in them to be more interesting, more challenging, and even more practical than the four-year high school. The one exception was geography, which stupidly was included in the sixth grade curriculum and ignored thereafter. What eleven-year-old gives a damn about the climate, products, people, and map shape of Afghanistan or even the state across the river from his own? On the other hand, by the time he becomes a junior or a senior in high school, his curiosity about the far corners of the world as well as his domestic neighbors usually has been whetted, to persist through college and the rest of his life, never to be satisfied completely.

Problems posed in elementary arithmetic could be solved by use of the purest form of logic, and I would have enjoyed my homework in that subject except for my curious inability to do fundamental addition and subtraction. I never could remember without great mental effort whether it is eight and seven that make fifteen or seventeen, or nine and eight that add up vice versa. Borrowing from integers and one-to-carry operations baffled me in adding and subtracting numbers. Thus, even after I had figured out logically how to solve one of those If-A-and-B problems I had to go through the elementary processes two or three times to get a correct answer. Frustrating.

In high school I found nothing whatever in algebraic equations and geometric theorems that was interesting, useful, or otherwise worth learning and remembering. So I exercised a useful talent for memorizing for brief retention, but learned nothing in those subjects—certainly not why the formulas worked. Physics, like arithmetic, had some engrossing aspects but chemistry was an abomination with all those combinations of elements, none of which had any lasting meaning except $H_2O$—and I never did comprehend how it was possible to combine two substances called gases and get a liquid. Some of the laboratory experiments had curious results but the most gratifying were those not mentioned in the textbooks.

All of the English courses were to my liking, but there was never enough of them and they were always incomplete. For some reason (a mental block, I suppose), I was never able to learn a single rule of grammar or to parse a sentence. I always wrote by ear—and I'm sure it showed. There was too much reading of Shakespeare at a too early age, and much later when I finally actually saw some of his plays performed I had an irritating feeling that nearly every line was plagiarized. That's been said before, I would remind myself; and of course it had been, by the Bard himself in the plays I had read.

Handwriting was a vexing problem; it is sometimes referred to in this machine age as a lost art, but for me it was never a found one. I could readily decipher my notebook hiero-glyphics but they were a meaningless code to others. When I was in high school, there was a typewriter in the second-floor office of the principal, who had no secretary. I learned a fast, two-finger hunt-and-peck system when I was in the ninth grade, and frequently devoted a study period to typing papers for the principal in payment for the privilege of using the machine to type my own notes into bits of composition on any subject that interested me at the moment.

I couldn't get to the typewriter, however, for the almost daily papers I had to turn in for classwork, or for monthly, midterm, and final examinations. These had to be readable by the teachers if I was to get the grades I wanted and thought I deserved; so in desperation I learned to draw letters rather than perfect Spencerian or some other favored form of pen-manship. It was slow but it worked. It got me through high school. At college and in my peripatetic career there was the portable typewriter.

I remember few men teachers, and the women were hardly dedicated feminine versions of Mr. Chips. Who could blame them? They were paid fifty to sixty dollars a month, and the young minds they encountered were seldom so promising as to inspire efforts at molding. Few of the teachers had college degrees; they were permitted to teach with two-year certificates from a state normal school. Most of them taught only long enough to pay for a trousseau needed for the marriage that was their real goal, one to be attained as soon as possible.

My sister was a grade behind me throughout school. Although she intended to teach, she had no ambition whatever for academic achievement in her own schooling; her aim was to make just passing marks so as not to be left behind to repeat a grade a second year. So, even though she was what Grandpa described as "bright as a dollar," she studied only enough to get by. Grandpa always looked at our report cards when we brought them home and nodded his head a few times without comment before passing them on to Grandma, who signed them. She sometimes praised me for high marks and chided Sis for her just-passing ones, but her main concern was that we stay in good health and out of trouble. We did both on the whole.

Sis was often teacher's pet despite her lackadaisical approach to learning, but I never rated any favoritism with my academic superiority. I argued too much with teachers and occasionally and unforgivably won an argument. Moreover, I relished baiting them, catching them in errors and blatting about them before the class. I think the descriptive phrase in use at the time for my type was a "damned young smart aleck."

I suppose it is natural in reviewing school days to recall the trivial triumphs and the scarring failures while forgetting the more important but routine events. At any rate the ones that come to my mind fall in the first two categories.

For example, I was always the best speller in school—or, at least, my classmates thought so, because the captains of the two teams appointed by the teacher for the Friday afternoon spelling bees always chose me when they got first pick by winning the coin toss. And I nearly always spelled down my opponents and was the last team member standing when the bee ended.

But, alas, when a Grayson team once challenged a team from Columbia to an interschool match I was spelled down on the third round. My humiliation was all the greater because the word I misspelled was "cotton." I spelled it "cotten"! Cotton was then almost the sole cash crop in the South and was the product that enabled my grandfather to rear and educate seven children of his own, then take over a repeat job with two grandchildren. And I couldn't spell the word. The humbling experience took much of the cockiness out of me, temporarily at least.

One of the clashes with teachers that did not endear me to them—this one was a man—also got Grandpa involved, how innocently on his part I never could decide.

The teacher had assigned for a brief homework essay the topic "Frankenstein the Monster." I reviewed the tale and said to Grandpa, "Say, this isn't right. Frankenstein wasn't the name of the monster but of the man who created him."

Grandpa nodded. "I suppose he meant the title of the paper to be 'Frankenstein's Monster' or 'The Frankenstein Monster.' But it's surprising how many people confuse the two, who think the name of the Monster was Frankenstein.

"It is also almost unbelievable how many misquoters there are in the world," he continued. "Just for fun, I'll give you some old sayings and literary allusions the way they are often wrongly quoted, in one way or another, sometimes changing the entire meaning. You write them down, show them to your teacher, and ask him if he thinks they are correct, or which ones are wrong and how. Then I'll tell you how they should be written—after I've done a little checking myself in Bartlett's," he concluded cautiously.

So he dictated and I wrote down whole sentences or fragments as follows:

1. Money is the root of all evil.
2. To gild the lily.
3. All present and accounted for.
4. Ignorance is bliss.
5. Music hath charms to soothe the savage beast.
6. Such stuff as dreams are made of.
7. All that glitters is not gold.
8. Hoist by his own petard.
9. The best laid plans of mice and men.
10. Water, water everywhere and not a drop to drink.
11. God rest you, merry gentlemen.

I took the sheet to Mr. Fletcher and asked him if he thought the quotations were correct, or if not, which ones were erroneous and in what way. He glanced over the eleven lines and handed the paper back to me.

"I see nothing wrong with them," he said impatiently. "That's the way I've always heard them or remembered them from reading."

I reported this to Grandpa. He laughed and said, "All right, I'll dictate the precise quotations, according to Bartlett's. Then you show them to your Mr. Fletcher and ask him if these versions ring a bell. I can't check all the original sources, because they range from the Bible to military manuals."

I made two lists, underlining certain significant words, one for Mr. Fletcher and one to keep, as follows:

1. *The love of* money is the root of all evil.
2. To *paint* the lily.
3. All present *or* accounted for.
4. *Where* ignorance is bliss.
5. Music hath charms to soothe the savage *breast*.
6. Such stuff as dreams are made *on*.
7. All that *glisters, glareth, glisteneth, or shineth*.
8. Hoist *with* his own *petar*.
9. The best laid *schemes o'* mice and men.
10. Water, water everywhere, *nor any* drop to drink.
11. God rest you merry, gentlemen.

When I gave Mr. Fletcher his copy, quoting my grandfather, who said *he* was quoting Bartlett's (I never got around to checking them all myself), he read the list through three times, getting progressively a little redder in the face. Then he crumpled the sheet and threw it away.

"Quibbles, quibbles, quibbles," he snorted, then asked contemptuously: "What college did your grandfather attend?"

"One you never heard of probably," I said impudently and not very originally. "The College of Hard Knocks."

Grandpa didn't laugh when I reported the outcome of his experiment.

"I probably shouldn't have done it," he said, "because you certainly don't need any help or encouragement in being smart-alecky. And that won't get you anywhere, in school or elsewhere."

Another assignment in English composition, when I was

in the tenth grade, changed the pattern of my life for years and was almost my undoing in the writing field. For a midterm examination the teacher wrote on the blackboard as the last of ten questions or assignments the following:

> Write a story in which the protagonist does something to reverse a situation and thereby accomplishes a purpose.

Whew! The teacher was just a country girl fresh out of college but with only a teaching certificate and no degree yet, and I am sure she knew nothing about the art of short story writing. She certainly hadn't taught any of its techniques in English composition, and I guessed she must have copied the sample assignment from some sort of teaching manual on the subject.

It was a challenge that might have given pause to Henri René Albert Guy de Maupassant, but not to his cocky sixteen-year-old disciple, who had read all his stories and every other one in that category of classics that he could find.

I devoted all of ten minutes to deep thought, then dashed off as rapidly as I could in my drawing-penmanship about twelve hundred words with a plot somewhat as follows:

A sixteen-year-old boy (who else?) who was very fond of animals and wanted a pet found a stray scrawny-looking kitten near his farm home one day. He showed it to his grandmother and begged to be allowed to keep it. Certainly not, said his grandmother sternly, not that awful-looking beast. Take it away and get rid of it somehow without hurting it. We can find you a more promising pet than that some day soon. . . . But the boy was both disobedient and sly. Instead of getting rid of the kitten, he hid it in the barn and every day managed to sneak out some milk and other food for it to eat in the barn. The kitten grew sleek and fat, and one day it got out of the barn somehow and was seen immediately by the grandmother. Here my boy, said the boy's unsuspecting guardian, is a real nice-looking, healthy kitten you may keep for a pet.

Aha! Assignment completed, mission accomplished. I wasn't quite sure what a protagonist was, but the boy in my tale sure as hell had done something to reverse a situation and thereby had achieved his own purpose, with a little help from coincidence. Of course, I knew of no such actual occurrence.

I was highly pleased with myself, especially when I saw my classmates sitting for half an hour or longer over "Exam Assignment No. 10," chewing on their pens and staring vacantly into space.

It turned out that no one else in the class had even attempted to write a story of any kind. The teacher was so flabbergasted that I had done so, at least readably, that she went overboard and gave me a mark of 100 on the exam paper, which it surely didn't deserve. Then, when the marked papers were returned, she kept mine long enough to read the story aloud to the class.

That was my ruination. As a result of that success in my first attempt at a short story (it actually was what came to be known by a few magazines a decade or two later as a short-short), I devoted much of my spare time for the next quarter of a century trying to become another O. Henry or Wilbur Daniel Steele. About a hundred manuscripts, twenty-five magazines, and six anthologies later, I sadly came to realize that my things were not true short stories, but tracts with tag-line morals, and that I was not really a creative writer but a re-creative one, if anything. When I think even now of all the things I might have been doing while I was slaving over a typewriter—

One memorable school incident had nothing to do with classwork. A short time before school opened when I was in one of the intermediate grades, I lost my footing while leaping to the top step of the back porch of the old Thompson house and skinned my left shinbone badly. Grandpa sent me to one of the two village doctors, Biggs or Hines, to have the injury treated and dressed.

For some reason it did not heal. It became infected, then a swollen mass of putrid flesh, such flesh as there is on a shin, and when I walked I limped with considerable pain. Uncle Robert, who then lived in Monroe and operated a profitable sanitarium there, came down for a weekend visit, and Grandpa asked him to do something about the injury. Uncle Robert was a very good physician; he did something to the sore that hurt like the dickens, dressed it with bandages extending from ankle to knee, and told Grandpa:

"That's a bad leg, and it could mean real trouble. He could even lose it. I'll come down again next weekend and I'll treat it again and put on new dressing. Meanwhile, keep the boy off his feet."

That was a sentence almost worse than death to me, because I knew Grandpa would obey instructions to the letter. Besides, it created a schooling problem. The new term was starting that week, and Grandpa didn't want me to miss out at the beginning. I didn't either.

The school was only about a quarter of a mile away, past our First House, past the old Grayson place, and down a short gravelly slope to the then unfenced campus and school buildings. Walking the distance meant I would have to be on my feet, and that was forbidden. So each morning Grandpa hoisted me onto Old Black's back and led the way to school, sparing activity on my bad leg. He came for me when school let out, and I rode home to sit quietly in a chair at a table until bedtime.

That took care of the morning and evening round trip, but

not the problem of dinner, the midday meal for which Sis and I were accustomed to rushing home. Many of the students who came to school in wagonettes from rural homes many miles away brought their lunches in pails and ate them cold during the noon recess while sitting under trees or on the outside back stairway to the second floor. But Grandpa believed a growing boy should have a hot meal in the middle of the day.

My class that year was assigned to a front room on the first floor and my desk happened to be directly beside a window rather high above the ground. It was always open at that time of year. Every school day for nearly three weeks, right on the dot at noon, a deep enamel pan with a capacity of about half a gallon would appear upon the window sill beside my desk. It contained a serving of everything set out for the noon meal on the Blackman table, and it was put there by Grandpa sitting astride Old Black (the saddle hadn't been discarded then). I ate my dinner, still warm, without leaving my seat.

Of course, I was not permitted to go out during the rest of the noon hour or at the morning and evening recesses, even to watch the other boys play prisoner's base, two-old-cat, and bullpen. That irked me no end, but as compensation I was relieved, at the grimly determined insistence of my grandfather member of the school board, of the field work that was a part of the curriculum of the agricultural high school.

The Grayson school had qualified for some badly needed federal aid under the Smith-Hughes Act and as a result boys in school received four credit units in agricultural subjects toward the required number for graduation, instead of in French, Latin, or other languages. The girls got four in domestic science, sometimes called home economics. Classes for both were held in a separate one-story building a little apart from the two-story main structure. The girls had a kitchen adjoining their classroom in which to get practice in the culinary arts they learned, but the boys had to go back of the campus to practice what had been preached, in a twenty-acre cultivated field and a complex of outbuildings for animal husbandry.

I suppose it was a good program for the community and for many of the students, but I didn't think it was for me. I got all the hoeing, plowing, fertilizing, planting, and harvesting skills I needed, and a great deal more than I wanted, at home. I wasn't interested in agronomy, or contour plowing to prevent erosion, or crop rotation, or legumes, or any other cover crops, or any allied subjects. I didn't want any part of farming.

Thus, I rejoiced that I not only was spared all of this for nearly three weeks but was excused from attending textbook classes in the Agriculture-Home Economics Building, because it meant a walk of about a hundred yards, going and coming, on my bad leg.

The agriculture teacher at that time was Professor A. J. (Fundy) Funderburk. He had married Katie Lee Howell, the elder sister of my first childhood sweetheart, who bore the name of Bill because her father had wanted a boy as a second child and stuck her with the masculine name he had chosen. It wasn't William, or Willie—just plain Bill.

The Funderburks were the proud parents of twin girls, the first ones born in Grayson to my knowledge, and I was awed the first time I saw them, because they were so tiny they both rested on a baby pillow with room to spare for a couple more. One of the twins, Marjorie, was destined to become the First Lady of Louisiana, wife of a Governor born in Grayson to the principal of the high school and his charming home economics teacher wife. No one dreamed then of such things coming to pass in the future, of course.

Before and after the bad leg reprieve, I conspired with other boys in his class to trick him into forgoing a dreary lecture or calling upon us to recite from assigned lessons. One of us would slyly bring up a controversial subject having nothing to do with agriculture by asking a seemingly innocent question at the start of the class period.

More often than not, Professor Fundy would rise to the bait and debate, devoting the entire forty minutes to expounding his views on a subject unrelated to his course. When dismissal time came, he would be so abashed at the realization that nothing had been taught or learned in that day's lesson that he would give each member of the class the same high mark. As a matter of fact, the impromptu discussions probably were of more lasting value than learning the textbook theories concerning the dynamiting of stumps in new ground and cross-pollination of hybrid corn by hand.

One school crisis that stands out in memory, because its resolution marked for me the end of one era and the beginning of another, also was only tangentially connected with education. It was a sartorial matter, akin to some of the current brouhahas over the hair styles and miniskirts of students.

One of the remembered delights of boyhood was going barefoot from early spring to late fall. I suppose the saving of shoe leather was a factor in the custom as far as parents were concerned, but that had nothing to do with the anticipation of a boy under teen-age of shucking his shoes and stockings when the weather got warm enough. The sensation produced by shuffling in loose soil the soles of bare feet tenderized by the wearing of coarse shoes all winter was almost erotic.

In a very short time of course the soles of bare feet became almost as coarse and thick as leather, impervious to briars, thistles, splinters, or anything less piercing than a rusty nail stepped upon in a plank or shingle. (Grease the nail immediately after withdrawing it from the stuck foot, Aunt Liza used to advise with more superstition than logic.)

Besides going barefoot all through summer vacation, I was accustomed to going shoeless to school in my short pants for at least a month each fall. This was what brought about the sartorial controversy.

In Grayson there was no such thing as graduation from elementary school—no commencement exercises, no diplomas, nothing of the sort. You simply finished the seventh grade on the first floor of the main building one spring and the next fall you went upstairs to the eighth grade classroom and the first year of high school. But when the time came for me to make the transition, I decided it was the occasion to shed short pants for long ones—peg-top trousers they were then, blousing outward for several inches just below the belt and tapering to cuffs so narrow the feet could hardly go through them and stopping a good four inches above the ankle. For my first day in high school I put on a pair of these trousers—but I went barefoot as usual, and this caused the commotion.

My sister said I looked silly. Grandpa paid no more attention to my attire than to his. Members of the faculty at school got into the act. My homeroom teacher said she wanted no long-pants barefoot students in her domain. The principal said it didn't matter. The girls were amused, the boys disinterested.

It was Grandma who put the quietus to all this conflict by issuing a rare edict:

"The shoes go on or the long pants come off. Can't wear one without the other. You're either still a boy, or you're not. Make up your mind."

I made up my mind. I kept wearing the long pants, and I put on shoes. I never went barefoot again. I was no longer a boy; if not yet a young man, I was at least an adolescent.

I felt a little sad. Never again would I know the joy of being Whittier's Barefoot Boy With Cheek of Tan, with his Blessings on a Little Man.

# XVI

There was no public library and no bookstore in Grayson. One of the general merchants stocked the textbooks that had to be bought each fall, but had no dealings with trade book publishing. In the school's study room there was a shelf of works for collateral reading in the English courses, most of them such heavy tomes as Plutarch's *Lives*. Grandpa once had amassed a fairly representative nonfiction collection, but gave away most of the volumes to his children when they got married and scattered several years before my sister and I came along.

He had kept or replaced a few standard stand-by reference works besides Bartlett's. They included an early edition of the original *World Almanac*, Fowler's *Modern English Usage*, Roget's *Thesaurus*, and Robert's *Rules of Order*.

(He made a point of explaining to me something that few people seem to know—that Robert was French, pronounced "Robair," and that it was incorrect to give credit for this guide to parliamentary proceedings to a nonexistent Roberts. "It's Robert in the singular with a possessive apostrophe *s*," he told me. "But not one person in a thousand spells or pronounces the title correctly. Such is fame. I suppose poor Robert profited little while he lived and he doesn't even get the credit due him now that he's dead." Grandpa erred on one point; Henry Martyn Robert lived to the age of eighty-six and did not die until 1923.)

I owned about a dozen worn and cherished volumes, most of them obtained by a rare mail order from the catalogue of a cut-rate house in New York. Uncle Robert—not pronounced Robair—thought Jane Porter's *Scottish Chiefs* and *Thaddeus of Warsaw* were the finest historical novels ever published and he gave me copies of both one Christmas.

In all of Grayson there were only two private libraries worthy of the designation. They were brought to town by families who had come within my memory from away up North in Tennessee. Each of these collections contained at least one hundred books, which seemed to me to be unimaginable literary wealth. One was owned by Brownie's family and the other by his next-door neighbors, the Cutlers.

Brownie boasted that he "never cracked a book" if he could avoid it. The Cutlers had long since read all the books they owned. Both families gladly permitted me to borrow at will from their shelves, and since doors were never locked in Grayson they urged me to help myself at any time without the formality of knocking.

I can recall few titles but I have the definite impression that both libraries represented either remarkably catholic tastes or very random methods of selection. The authors ranged from Alger to Shakespeare and included both Zane Grey and Rudyard Kipling types of fiction.

As for me, I had no discrimination whatever; anything printed between covers was food and nectar to my insatiable appetite for reading. My method of selection was simple. I started with the first three books on the left of the top shelf at Brownie's house and read my way across that and each of the lower shelves. I took three home twice a week and when I had finished all at Brownie's I shifted to the Cutlers' and did the same there. After I had devoured both collections I started all over again.

After the fourth round, I began to tire of the same literary adventures, and it was about that time that I made a great discovery. One movie night in Clarks, I stopped as I entered the auditorium to look through a window of the library operated by the lumber company at the front of the building. I saw people of all ages reading at long tables. There were yards and yards of shelves around three walls, all stacked with rows of books in sections that were labeled in large letters. I ventured inside to expore this veritable "Treasure Island."

My first impulse was to start reading indiscriminately with the first book on the left of the top shelf, but after half an hour of delirious browsing, I decided that with so much riches at hand I could be selective. So I chose a book with an author familiar to me, found an unoccupied chair at a table and began to read.

The Clarks library was open from 5 to 10 P.M. each day except Sunday, and for the next two weeks I was there every night shortly after six o'clock, the movies forgotten. I couldn't get there any earlier after supper even when I reluctantly rode Old Black. I didn't like the walk and I begrudged the time it required. The evening trains were a bit late going and too early returning for the library schedule. So I usually imposed on the old horse, when he wasn't too tired; I would hitch him to a tree back of the old Community Center for the four hours I lived in other worlds inside. It mattered little to him where he was; he could sleep on his feet anywhere.

At that time I knew nothing about the operation of public libraries. I saw people sitting and reading at the tables and I assumed that was the only privilege accorded to patrons. In time, I noticed that certain people came in, left books at the librarian's desk, chose others from the shelves, and took them out with them after pausing to let the librarian check them.

I was curious about this procedure; I had read about library cards but understood only dimly how they were used. For the first two weeks I was too enchanted to make inquiries. I was usually so absorbed, in fact, that the librarian, a pale, tired woman whose name I never learned, had to tap my shoulder after she had tapped a bell to announce closing time.

One night I couldn't find in its place on the shelf the book I had been reading the night before, so I chose another. When the librarian reminded me personally that it was time to leave, I asked, "What happened to the book I was reading last night? *Hans Brinker*, it was."

"I suppose someone took it out to read at home," she said.

"Took it out?" I asked. "How do you do that?"

She looked at me for a long moment.

"Didn't you know that you can sign a card and use it to

take out as many as three books at a time to keep for a month and read at home?"

"No ma'am," I said. "I wondered—"

She looked at her watch. "Well, come over to the desk," she said, "and I'll make out a card for you now."

Elated and thinking how glad Old Black would be if he could know of this development, I followed her to the desk.

"What's your name?" she asked, poising a pen over a card. I told her.

"Where do you live?"

"In Grayson," I said.

Slowly, she put down her pen and studied me. "Do you mean to say that you've been coming down here from Grayson every night just to sit and read for a few hours?"

"Why, yes, ma'am. It doesn't take long to get here. I ride our old horse most nights."

"And when you don't ride the horse, how do you get here? Walk?"

"Yes'm. I don't mind the walk so much, but it cuts down on my reading time and makes me kinda late getting home."

She looked at the card, on which she had made one notation. Her speech was a little confusingly pedantic when next she spoke:

"Marion Blackman, I'm sorry to tell you that this benevolent lumber yard company for which I work does not recognize the existence much less the mental starvation of anyone who does not live in Clarks. This library is not for you, except for reading on the premises as you have been doing. I'm very sorry."

"You mean—?"

"I mean that I cannot give you a lending card. I try every day to force them upon dolts and dullards who work for the lumber company, or whose relatives do, but under the rules I am not permitted to lend books to anyone who lives outside the paternalistic pale of the company town, no matter how deserving or wishful he may be to receive such benefits."

"That's all right, ma'am," I said awkwardly. "I don't mind coming down here to read. You're sure that's all right under the rules?" I asked anxiously.

"It certainly is," she said emphatically. "And if some lumber lord decides to change the rules to keep you out, he'll have to get a new librarian." She tore the card I wasn't to get into small pieces and dropped them in a wastebasket. "Good night, Marion. Closing time."

A few nights later, the librarian, looking a bit less pale and tired than usual, beckoned me to her desk when I entered.

"Welcome, new citizen of Clarks," she said mystifyingly. "I hope you enjoy your new residence in our town."

"What's that mean?" I asked. "I haven't moved to Clarks. I can't, because—I mean—"

"Clarks has moved to you, in a manner of speaking," she said, smiling faintly. "Yesterday, I bearded the General Superintendent in his den. I had never been there before, and I was encouraged to note that its walls were well-lined with books. When I left, the corporate literary boundaries of Clarks had been extended by fiat to include your corner of the bookless wasteland of Grayson."

I got lost in this rhetorical maze, but there was no mistaking the meaning of her abrupt concluding sentence.

"Here's your library card."

I went home early that night, taking three books with me. Old Black rested for several nights, then took me back to the Clarks library where I returned the first three and checked out three more.

This routine was followed thereafter as long as I lived in Grayson, which an understanding lumber company librarian had managed to include—by literary gerrymander—in her domain.

# XVII

---

Temptations for youthful wrongdoers seem to exist in every community and all periods, differing somewhat in kind and degree, of course. I don't think I ever committed a real crime or did anything that could be called truly wicked, but I got into my share of scrapes as a boy. I recall four of them chiefly in the light of my grandfather's reaction to them. This was generally one of tolerance and understanding, but I regret one escapade, because I don't think he ever quite forgave me for it. This was not a result of his disapproval of the misdemeanor itself, a petty theft, but because I lied about it and never admitted the truth.

The earliest misfeasance that comes to mind also was a theft—of an automobile. That sounds a bit grave, but it really was unintentional and grew out of a chain of circumstances over which I had some control but failed to exercise it.

Like most small boys, I was fascinated by cars, which in my time were just coming into general use, but not by the horse-and-slide Blackmans. The first auto in Grayson was a thing called a Motor-Go Buggy and it was owned by Dr. Biggs. It looked like a buggy without shafts. Its one- or two-cylinder motor was started (not on every attempt) with a detachable crank inserted on the left side near the step giving access to the single seat. It was steered with a tiller somewhat like that of the later electrics.

The Motor-Go Buggy ran seldom and never very far. It was towed about as many miles as it ran under its own power, and eventually it was left to rot on its solid rubber tires in the side yard of the Biggs home.

Dr. Biggs was an enthusiastic automobilist, however, perhaps because he had a lame leg requiring the use of a single crutch. He bought new and better models as they came out. His eldest son, Henley (with a nickname, "Doc," that he disliked), was a year younger than I but a good friend. I envied him because Dr. Biggs taught him to drive when he was still a small boy.

By the time Dr. Biggs had acquired a fairly dependable Overland roadster, Henley was doing most of the driving for his father when not in school. Sometimes he invited me to go along on professional trips when his father was in a good humor.

Dr. Biggs was rather gruff in manner, so I never dared ask him to let me have a try at driving, and since Henley was not then allowed to take the car out alone, I had no chance to learn under his tutelage. But I memorized the motions of driving by watching Henley and the doctor on the rare occasions when the latter took the wheel. The Overland had a standard shift and I visualized the gear mechanism as having the shape of the letter H, with the crossbar representing neutral and the other sections serving as channels for shifting into reverse, low, second, and high gears. I also noted the alternating functions of the clutch pedal and the gas lever in the shifting of gears.

I went through these motions so often in my mind that I was thoroughly convinced I could drive as well as Henley and perhaps better than the doctor. I yearned for the opportunity to prove this and when it unexpectedly came I was too obsessed to give thought to the consequences.

Henley had invited me along on a trip to Columbia, where Dr. Biggs replenished his supplies of drugs that he prescribed and also sold in the village's one drugstore. After the doctor had limped into the supply house on his crutch that day, Henley went off on an errand of his own, leaving me alone in the car.

The motor was running, because the Overland had no self-starter and gasoline was regarded as cheaper than the elbow grease required for hand cranking. This presented a temptation that was too strong for me to resist, and one thing inevitably led to another.

I intended at first only to ease the car forward a few feet in low gear and then back up to its original parking position. But the first operation went off so smoothly that I automatically continued through the rest of the motions, shifting into second and then into high gear. By the time this was accomplished, I had reached a cross street and, somewhat panicky, decided to drive around the block and park again in front of the supply house in the hope that neither the doctor nor Henley had returned to find me and the Overland missing.

Unfortunately, I had forgotten for a moment that it was not possible to go around that block. The side street debouched into the main highway, which to the right led across the river bridge and to the left went to Grayson. I turned left, judging that to be a lesser evil than crossing the bridge.

By now, I was both frightened and exhilarated. The car steered easily and responded like a thing alive to my unskilled touch. But I knew I had to stop soon and go back, somehow.

The gravel-surfaced highway was too narrow to turn around on, and I came to no other intersection. There seemed to be nothing I could do except stop and abandon the car, go back and confess my guilt; or drive on in the hope that I would come to a place wide enough for a turnaround. If I could do the latter, there was still a chance that I could get the car back where it should be without being detected as a thief.

I drove on, climbed a long hill, and about half a mile out of Columbia came to a spot that looked wide enough for turning. Well, it wasn't. Not for a driver of my inexperience. As I clumsily maneuvered the Overland toward the edge of the road, it eased over into a wide and shallow ditch, and I was stuck. I couldn't go forward, because of a fence, and when I tried to back up, the motor stalled. I couldn't start it again.

I don't know how long I cranked and cried but through exhaustion and tears I hardly recognized Henley when he came toiling up the hill on foot. Whether intuition or a tip from a passing motorist brought him there, he never told me. He didn't say a word at the time, and I was unable to speak at all. He adjusted the spark and gas levers, cranked furiously until the motor started with a roar, and then got behind the wheel and backed easily out of the ditch. He drove off down the hill to Columbia and I started walking to Grayson.

Twenty minutes later, the Overland whizzed by me in a cloud of gravelly dust, with Dr. Biggs looking stonily ahead and Henley cutting his eyes sidewise at me as he drove past.

I had walked from Columbia to Grayson many times, but on this occasion I suffered mental agony at every step. I was not only appalled at my recklessness and stupidity, but I could think of no remotely reasonable explanation of my conduct to Grandpa.

In the last mile, I decided not to tell him, in the forlorn hope that Dr. Biggs would not mention my misdeed to him or anyone else who might carry tales.

In the dreadful days that followed, I avoided Dr. Biggs and Henley and waited apprehensively for Grandpa to bring up the subject. Nearly a week later, when I had almost reached the conclusion that Dr. Biggs had remained charitably silent, Grandpa spoke brusquely to me:

"Son, I told Otis Biggs that you didn't mean to steal his fool automobile, because you are not a thief at heart. But I also told him that I was sure that never again would you borrow anybody's property without permission just to find out how it functions. Right?"

"Right!" I said fervently.

It was a different peck of trouble with the stolen pears.

Mr. Hendricks owned the farm just north of the old Thompson place, and his house was just beyond the fence separating the two properties. Between the fence and his house I saw one day a young pear tree laden with ripening fruit. It was the tree's first crop, and the total number of pears hanging from the limbs, all within reach from the ground, probably was no more than a dozen. Mr. Hendricks was proud of that tree, and I had heard him boasting to Grandpa that the pears looked as big and juicy and delicious as any he had ever seen on larger and older trees. He said he was looking forward to picking them soon, when they had ripened to just the right point, and he was going to share them as dessert with Mrs. Hendricks and perhaps give a couple to his son, Tom, and his new daughter-in-law.

Well, it was I and not Mr. Hendricks who picked the pears from the young tree. I had an accomplice, but it was my wicked idea and I had no motive. I actually cared less for pears than almost any other fruit and I knew full well how Mr. Hendricks treasured them. Wes, the Negro boy with whom I sometimes worked and played around our place, was still there after dark one evening.

"Let's go over to the Hendricks place and steal those big ripe pears off his young tree," I proposed.

"What for?" Wes asked reasonably. "You like pears that good, why don't you eat some out of your grandpappy's old orchard?"

"They're not as good," I said.

"How do you know? You ain't tasted either one."

"Oh, shut up and come on," I ordered.

I suppose the real thrill, if it could be called such, lay in the fact that while we noiselessly stripped the tree of its fruit we could see Mr. and Mrs. Hendricks through an open window not twenty feet away, placidly rocking and unsuspectingly reading in a lighted room.

The rest of the adventure was a stupid anticlimax. We ate one pear each and threw the rest away. We had never done anything like that before. We had stolen watermelons on moonlit nights without really hungering for them, but we never took more than the one we could eat, and the owner of the melon patch wouldn't have minded if he had known. This pear thing was pure wantonness, and I had the grace to be ashamed of myself.

I suppose that was why I lied when Grandpa confronted me with the accusation.

"Somebody stole all the pears from that young tree Mr. Hendricks has been tending all summer," Grandpa said. "He says you did it."

"What makes him think I did it?" I asked, side-stepping.

"I didn't ask him," Grandpa said coldly. "I'm asking you: Did you steal his pears?"

"No, sir," I lied stoutly.

"Are you sure you're telling the truth? You were out last night after supper and you had the opportunity."

"I'm sure."

"I can understand a boy's petty thievery," Grandpa said. "But I can't stand a liar."

"I'm not a liar," I insisted.

"Mr. Hendricks says he wouldn't have sold those pears for any amount of money, but they were worth fifty cents on the market. He claims I owe him fifty cents. Do I?"

"You don't owe him anything," I protested, "because I didn't steal his old pears."

Grandpa said no more then and never spoke of the incident again after one brief, cold, revealing statement two days later.

"I paid Mr. Hendricks his fifty cents," he told me, and walked away, his face as stern as his voice had been harsh, and his back rigid.

I knew then. I had lied, and somehow he knew it. He wanted me to know that he knew I had lied. He could have forgiven the theft but I don't think he ever forgave the lie.

It was the only one he ever had to forgive or not to forgive. I never lied to him again.

Two other escapades involved girl trouble, and Grandpa's reactions were mixed but on the whole comforting. One occurred before I reached the age of puberty, and I was guilty of nothing more heinous than puppy love and stupidity. The second was my adolescent initiation in sex experience with a girl, and I learned a couple of things no male can know too early.

I have mentioned that my first childhood sweetheart was a classmate, Bill Howell, who, I must admit, showed little awareness of the place she held in my affections. We paired off in boy-and-girl school events when I could arrange it without much cooperation from her, and I even went calling upon her at her home a few times, if such a term can be used in describing visits that only I persisted in thinking of as courtship. She probably was not even pretty in a conventional sense, but she was small for her age, and I think the word most often used to describe her was "cute."

Thinking of her one night after I had gone to bed, a longing to see her right then became so acute that I got up, dressed, slipped out of the house, and went down the railroad track to her home. I knew where she slept, and there was a lighted window in her bedroom. I crept up to the window, which was open, and looked in.

She had taken off her dress preparatory to putting on night-clothes, whatever kind she wore. There was nothing enticing for a peeping tom to see, if that had been my purpose. She still had on a pair of those voluminous things called bloomers and an underwaist of some sort to cover nonexistent breasts. I wasn't interested in looking at anything other than her face, anyway. I stood stupidly just outside the window through which the light shone, making no attempt at concealment but not making known my presence either. I must have made some movement, however, for suddenly she looked in my direction, startled and even frightened. She turned and ran out of the room.

I was on the point of leaving when the beam of a flashlight shone in my face, and I heard Mr. Howell say, "What the devil are you doing here, peeping in my girl's window and scaring the daylights out of her?"

I didn't answer. Instinctively, I turned and ran like a deer in the bright moonlight across a pea patch. I could hear Mr. Howell in close pursuit. With him was Mrs. Howell, for I heard her cry:

"Don't shoot, Sebe! After all, he's just a boy in knee pants."

I ran smack into a ten-foot chicken wire fence that I couldn't climb and saw no way of going around. I fell among the pea vines and lay there trembling until Mr. Howell growled, "Get out of there, get up, and come along with me."

I got up, and for my benefit he aimed the flashlight in his left hand at the automatic pistol he carried in his right, then turned it on my face.

"Why, it's Marion Blackman!" Mrs. Howell exclaimed.

I walked ahead of them back to the house, where he ordered me to sit on the front steps. Bill must have been dying of curiosity but she didn't appear. I don't remember how Mr. Howell got word to my grandfather, but after what seemed a horribly interminable period, Grandpa suddenly was there. He and Mr. Howell went off to one side and talked in under-tones that I could not make out until finally he said aloud:

"All right, Mr. Howell, just leave the punishment to me." Then he came over and said, "Come along, Son."

He never punished me. He didn't even rebuke me. On the way home, he asked:

"Lying there in bed, you got to thinking about that little girl. Right?"

"Yes, sir."

"And you wanted real bad to see her right then?"

"Yes, sir."

"So instead of waiting for a suitable time, you got up and dressed and went down to her house just to see her. Is that the way it was?"

"That's just what happened."

"You didn't have anything else in mind?"

"No, sir, I didn't. I swear I didn't."

"No need to swear."

That was all he said on the subject except, as usual, he could not resist the opportunity to point up a little lesson he thought I might learn from the misadventure.

"You'll find out sooner or later that quite often when you start thinking about something it's wiser just to go on thinking instead of doing something about it right then and there. Not always, of course," he added. "Obeying that impulse is the way many worthwhile things get done."

Even though he didn't mention the event again, that didn't mean I had heard the last of it. Mr. Howell couldn't refrain from telling the tale around town, and for weeks I was the target of lewd gibes by the idlers occupying the benches in front of the post office-barbershop building. They made my life miserable until another "scandal" came along to occupy their attention.

Bill herself looked me over curiously the next time we met, but had no comment. Thereafter, we were just classmates, pretty good friends, and that suited both of us. In high school days I even had a few casual dates with her, and no objections were raised by her parents, whatever they thought. Bill had other boyfriends, of course, and the last I heard of her she had been happily married to a man in Jena. . . . I wish her continued happiness.

Like Bill, I had other sweethearts, but the girl who initiated me into the mystery of sex was not one of them. She was Everybody's Girl. To borrow a phrase from one of Erskine Caldwell's *Tobacco Road* characters, she was always a-horsing. She wasn't a prostitute; the thought of taking money probably never occurred to her. She was just promiscuous, always ready and willing and capable. The word got around, of course, among the young bucks, and they took turns, some regularly, many only occasionally, and a few like me only once.

It should have been a red-letter day (or night), but I can't remember exactly how old I was when my turn came. But I was old enough and according to the studies by the late Dr. Kinsey I was more than ready—I was eager.

I took the girl, whom I'll call Lois, home from a Wednesday night prayer meeting in the Baptist church across the railroad from where I lived. The chief drawback to an affair with Lois was that she lived a long dark mile deep into an area of second-growth pines. A dim, winding wagon trail led through those forbidding woods to the dismal farmhouse she shared with a large family, none of whom paid much attention to her and either didn't know or didn't care about her sexual adventures.

I enjoy good earthy bawdiness if it's funny, but I've never been very good at it myself. So I will skip the details of my initiation.

I will record only that our bed of dalliance was a layer of dead pine needles beside the wagon road half way to her home. She was experienced but not so proficient as to cope adeptly with my clumsiness; so the act was a disappointment to me and almost certainly unsatisfactory to her.

It was the aftermath that was shameful on my part. The seemingly inevitable male reaction after I was spent amounted almost to revulsion, and I wanted cravenly only to get away.

"Look, Lois," I said sheepishly and half apologetically, "I think I better be getting home. You can make it the rest of the way by yourself, can't you?"

"I could," she said, "but I won't. Listen, Marion," she went on gently after the fashion of Grandpa teaching a lesson, "you got to learn some day and you might as well know now that women are different from men. They want attention both before and after they do it, especially afterward. It keeps them from feeling like they're just being used, like they are wanted for other things than just rolling around on pine needles until the man is satisfied. So you're going to walk me home and if you got any sense you'll always do something like that for every female you ever have anything to do with."

I didn't realize then that I was hearing instinctive words of wisdom from a country girl courtesan but I was chastened. I walked her home. In silence. I couldn't think of anything to say, and she had made already probably the longest speech of her life. But I kissed her on the forehead when I said good night at the creaky old front gate.

"Good night, Lois, and thank you," I said awkwardly, not quite knowing why I was saying it. "For everything and especially for what you told me."

I meant it even if I didn't quite know why and I often thought of her words later.

The consequence of my first experience was alarming, to say the least. I learned of the situation from Grandpa, who as I have noted always managed in one way or another to be aware of what was going on in the village.

"It seems that sort of wild young girl they call Lois who lives out there in the woods west of town is going to have a baby," he told me. "The police jury is investigating, and somebody is going to have to marry her, or else."

"Is that so?" I asked inanely.

"She apparently doesn't know who's the father," Grandpa went on, "but she gave a list of suspects, shall we call them, to the police jury. I understand it's quite a long list, a dozen or so names, and interestingly enough they are in alphabetical order."

I didn't say anything.

"Apparently no A names were involved," Grandpa continued relentlessly. "So the list begins with B names. And I am reliably informed that the first name on the list is Blackman. There are only two male Blackmans in town and I rather doubt she had me in mind when she made out her list."

"Well, sir, I don't know about—I can't say what the others—" I came to a stammering halt.

"Couldn't you have waited a while for that experience?" Grandpa said evenly. "What was the hurry? With luck you should have fifty years ahead of you for that sort of thing after you get married. Don't you think that's enough, and don't you think the woman you marry has as much right to expect certain things from you as you will expect from her?"

"I guess so," I murmured, embarrassed and unconvinced.

"You've got a more immediate problem to worry about right now, unless this Lois narrows her list or makes a choice, or somebody in the group that enjoyed her favors volunteers to do right by her. As number one on the list, are you ready to get married at your age?"

"I sure ain't," I said inelegantly but fervently.

"Well, there's nothing to do now but wait," he said.

We waited, and the police jury sent word to those on the list to come to Columbia for questioning. But sighs of relief were heard in a dozen homes in Grayson and environs when the situation was saved by a volunteer before the questioning could begin, one of the possible solutions suggested by Grandpa.

This hero, one of the regulars, obviously cared enough for Lois not to be disturbed by her failure to care only for him. Besides, I heard later, he believed in his heart that he was the father. Anyway, he married her and the baby was born in wedlock. Without any knowledge or gossip about their married life to form an opinion, I would wager that Lois was a faithful wife to the bumpkin that married her.

But again Grandpa had to sound a warning with a moral:

"There may not be a volunteer to come forward and take the blame and the responsibility the next time, so you'd better see to it there is no next time."

I didn't make any promises, and that's all I care to say on that subject.

# XVIII

One summer I chopped cotton for a farmer neighbor who paid me fifty cents a day—and what a day's work it was. Field hands were expected to be on the job from can to can't, and in summer that meant a good twelve hours. Chopping cotton is a meaner business than hoeing corn. The stand of stalks (a few inches high at chopping time) has to be thinned so that those that remain will have space and sufficient soil around them to grow properly. Quite often when the layer of grass and topsoil is chopped away the stalks are so frail they collapse unless they are hilled up, generally by hand, and that is tedious work.

I had a definite financial goal—the sum of eight dollars—and I stuck it out for sixteen days. The farmer grumbled as he paid me off because I was quitting before the field was finished, but I had had it.

Eight dollars was the price an older boy I knew was asking for the bicycle he had outgrown. It wasn't much of a bike. He had inherited it from his older sister, which meant that it was a girl's bike. This differed from a boy's in that it had no cross rod extending from the seat to the handlebars. It was considered unseemly in those times for a female to sit astride anything. A girl's bike was less sturdy but I found the absence of the bar averted groin injury when a sudden stop forced unexpected dismounting. The leather seat was about the size of a man's hand and had no spring. The frame was painted blue, which I thought was a sissy color, instead of a robust red. But it cost only eight dollars and I doubted that I'd ever amass the twenty-five that a new boy's bike would have cost.

Ignoring the jeers of my friends and my sister's hints that it properly should become hers, I rode that old girl's bike the rest of the summer, fall and winter. Then in the spring I set my sights on a new goal; I saw a possible way to earn twenty-five dollars for a new bike.

A 4-H Club sponsored at school devised projects for each member. Some raised a hog or a calf and some grew cotton or potatoes or another cash crop. I elected to plant an acre of corn because Grandpa had the seed and the old Thompson place included an acre-size field of newground fertile enough, I thought, to yield at least twenty-five barrels of corn.

That was important since the going market value of corn then was a dollar a barrel—if a buyer could be found at any

price. I worried aloud about that until to my joy Grandpa
proposed a deal.

"Tell you what I'll do," he said. "If you can coax twenty-
five barrels of good corn from that piece of newground, I'll
buy it from you at a dollar a barrel."

"You will? Sure enough? That would fix me up just fine."

"It will mean hard work," he cautioned, "and you'll be on
your own. I won't even give you advice. You'll have to decide
when to flat-break the land, when to plow the rows, when to
plant, and hoe. You probably should fertilize and that means
collecting and scattering manure, because you won't have the
money for commercial fertilizer."

"I know where to find cow and chicken manure and I'll do
it," I said confidently.

"Remember now," Grandpa warned, "if you fall short of
the twenty-five barrels, it's no bargain. You'll have to find
another market for a lesser yield. My buying it will be to
reward you for good work in getting the most out of the
land."

"There may be a bigger yield," I boasted.

"I'll buy all you can grow this season on that acre," Grandpa promised.

Never was a tract of land cultivated so assiduously as was
my acre that spring and summer. I flat-broke the land with
Old Black and a turn plow. I used the slide and a couple of
barrels to collect manure from every cow pen and chicken
roost in the area. I scattered it and harrowed it under. Then
I laid out the rows and used the turn plow again to throw
them up. A narrow shovel blade opened the furrows and since
seed was plentiful I dropped more than a good stand so it
could be selectively thinned at hoeing time to proper spaces
between stalks. I had never paid any attention to growing corn

before, but when mine came up a healthy green I thought I had never seen a more beautiful sight.

Until midsummer I fought every weed and blade of grass that dared poke itself above ground in my cornfield, using a middlebuster between rows and a hoe between stalks. When my crop was laid by to continue its growth to maturity with two or three ears of corn to the stalk, it was clean of all noxious plants. . . . I kept a record of all this for the 4-H Club.

The mixture of rain and sunshine that summer was just right for corn, and mine grew tall and green. I watched it tassel and put out ears with silks peeping from the tips of the shucks, then turn harvest brown. When the cornsilk was dark and dry enough to be rolled into cigarettes and smoked, I knew it was time to gather my corn.

This I did in less than a day, pulling the ears and throwing them unshucked into a box on the slide drawn between the rows by Old Black. I hauled the crop to the barn and measured the first load, learning that the box held three barrels even.

Grandpa was there smiling when I came in with my tenth and last load, and he gave a cheer when I showed him the total. My acre had yielded thirty full barrels—plus a few extra ears which I fed to Old Black.

After supper that evening Grandpa handed me six five-dollar bills and made his shortest comment ever on anything I had done.

"Good work, Son," he said.

Well, now I could buy the bright-red boy's bike I had long coveted, but a momentous choice had to be made: what make? All bikes on the market were very much alike in the essentials, differing in types of coaster brakes, tires, seats, handlebars, mudguards, and accessories. I studied the catalogues and considered this feature and that; I liked one thing on a certain make, another thing on a second, and something else on a third.

A novel thought occurred to me. Why not buy a frame and the various parts separately and put together my own custom-made bicycle?

I knew this was feasible, since there was in Shreveport a large shop that sold not only several makes but all sorts of bicycle parts. I figured I had five dollars more than was needed to put together a dream bike; I would use this to visit Uncle Robert and Aunt Birdie in Shreveport, make my purchases, assemble the machine, and ride it back to Grayson. It was only about a hundred miles and I estimated I could make it in a couple of days easily, camping out for one night.

Grandpa thought about it for a while, then gave permission. The next morning I rode the northbound to Monroe and changed there to a train on the V.S. & P. for the second leg of the trip to Shreveport.

I had the time of my life assembling that bike and nearly drove a salesman out of his mind. After trying first one thing and then another, I finally decided on a New Departure coaster brake, longhorn cattle handlebars with special rubber handgrips, light but strong tires, an oversize seat with good springs—this from one make, that from another, and so on. It was close figuring; eliminating all accessories, I got back some change from my five-dollar bills.

I proudly rode my custom-built beauty out to Uncle Robert's house, stowed it in a corner of the porch behind a swing, and went to bed early so I could start the homeward ride at dawn.

It was the worst day that had ever dawned for me. My fine new dream bike was gone! Stolen during the night. Irrevocably gone.

There was no use reporting the theft to the police, for as

Uncle Robert pointed out my put-together machine didn't even have a serial number. It was certainly distinctive enough for identification, but it could have been dismantled as readily as it had been assembled and the various components probably would be sold by the thief as soon as the repair shops opened.

"Darn fool thing to do anyway," Uncle Robert said unfeelingly. "Riding a bicycle overland a hundred miles."

Grandpa was sympathetic and did not reproach me for my carelessness in not guarding against thieves. He remarked:

"I suppose you must be thinking that Christ was crucified in *really* bad company."

That dream bike was the last I ever owned. It rode fine while I had it.

# XIX

Boys and girls in my time did not "go steady" to the extent that seems to be the custom today, and as I have already indicated attachments were formed and dissolved frequently and easily until the time came to think seriously of marriage. There were exceptions, of course.

My junior year sweetheart was a sophomore named Marilee, and she was the heroine of a box supper that was the first I ever attended with both money in my pocket and love in my heart. The box supper was the favored form of charity benefit in Grayson. The women and girls prepared the containers of viands, which were offered anonymously (in theory) for sale at auctions held at the school or a church, and the men and boys did the bidding at prices far above the cost or worth of the contents. After all the boxes had been disposed of to the highest bidders, the buyers shared the suppers with the females who had prepared them and whose identities had been revealed by one means or another before the bidding began. The proceeds went to whatever needy cause in the community was most pressing at the time.

The boxes themselves ranged from plain cardboard oblongs to wondrous creations of imaginative design and mysterious construction. The contents, however, varied little. They consisted of fried chicken, baked ham, or some other meat that could be relished cold; two or three kinds of salad, always including potato; several relishes; pie, cake, and fruit. Portions were large. Their quality was seldom a surprise to the buyer, as the culinary accomplishments of most of the older women were pretty well known in the community, and their daughters' boxes also could be rated accordingly.

The sale of the boxes contributed by the matrons was cut-and-dried, and occasioned little interest. When the offerings of a married woman came up, she customarily gave her husband alongside her in the audience a dig in the ribs, whereupon he dutifully bid a generous one dollar, the going rate for connubial suppers out of a box for charity, and that was that. It sometimes happened that a couple of husbands got their signals mixed, or their wives recognized a wrong box. The misunderstanding would be settled amicably though, for the couples would sup together, sharing the contents of both boxes and trying to outdo each other with compliments.

For the younger element the box supper was something else again, an event in which they took part with subdued excitement and which their observant and sometimes anxious parents watched with varying emotions. It was a catalytic social agent; it started youthful romances, it intensified them, and sometimes it ended them.

Most of the proceeds from these box suppers resulted from the bids of the courting, marriageable, and prideful swains involved in the ever-changing pattern of rivalries over the belles of the town. Sometimes even the plainest girls, if they (or their mothers) were known to be good cooks, inspired lively bidding among the reckless youths who were callous to romance but had lusty appetites and felt charitable. Now and then one of these high bids with low motives led to happy marriages and a satisfying confirmation of the truth of the old adage about the way to a man's heart being through his stomach.

When I made my debut as a solvent and romantic participant, I had one known rival, Brownie-across-the-railroad, my old Christmas fireworks competitor. During the previous summer I had worked in his father's small lumbermill, where Brownie was a sort of straw boss. At that time he had had no interest in Marilee, nor had he known how I felt about her. Nevertheless, he had lorded it over me and made my life miserable with a score of petty tyrannies. Our relationship, always volatile, was not exactly cordial at summer's end.

After we returned to school late in September, I inadvertently revealed to him my feeling for Marilee. Motivated by pure perversity, Brownie thereupon began chasing her too. In turn, he was being pursued shamelessly by a girl named Belle who lived down the street from him. Brownie ostentatiously spurned Belle and courted Marilee. Being somewhat more naïve in these matters than he, I didn't realize that Brownie was simultaneously spurring Belle's interest in him and making me suffer in a sadistic extension of our summer differences. I began almost to hate him, an emotion that would have left him completely unmoved if he had been aware of it.

The day of the box supper, Marilee gave me the clues to recognition of her box: It would be square, wrapped in green tissue, tied with a red ribbon, and adorned with a spray of bachelor's-buttons. I had saved eight dollars from my summer's part-time work, and on the fateful evening I was prepared to bid two dollars, or even as high as three, to obtain Marilee's culinary prize and much more desired company. I felt obliged to hold out at least five dollars for a light topcoat; if I didn't, I would have to go without one through a winter that could be counted upon to have its cold spells. I then was buying most of my clothes with money earned in the summer labor market, because Grandpa's capital and INTEREST were both diminishing for economic or other reasons beyond my knowledge or concern.

The auctioneer at this particular box supper, held in the school auditorium, was a horse trader named Albert Toomis, an uncle of the Belle who was enamored of Brownie. He stood on the platform, his right hand holding a gavel and his left holding aloft each box as it was handed to him by an assistant sitting at a stacked table. His spiel was a combination of excessive gallantry toward the women and challenging joviality toward the men. On this evening, as usual, he began by getting a lot of easy laughs from the audience, in none of which I joined. It was a serious occasion for me.

I sat a few seats to the left of the center aisle, in the third row. Sis, who knew of my romantic and economic intention, sat directly behind me. She had brought no box, since she shared the view of our absent grandparents that the entire concept of the box supper was a nonsensical if harmless subterfuge for straightforward donations for charity. As custom dictated, Marilee sat elsewhere pending my successful bid for her company at supper.

I paid little attention to the proceedings until at last Mr. Toomis held up a square green box with a red ribbon and a readily identifiable spray of bachelor's buttons.

Nervously fingering the little wad of bills in my pocket, I opened my mouth to say a vigorous "One dollar!" Instead, I heard "Three dollars!" and it was not my voice saying it. Across the aisle I spotted Brownie, wickedly watching me out of the corner of one eye. He must have obtained somehow, probably from a girl friend of Marilee, a description of her box.

Outraged by his tactic, I blurted, "Four dollars!" (There went a dollar out of my five-dollar coat fund.)

Behind me, Sis whispered hoarsely, "Oooh, you fool!" I didn't look around.

After this unheard-of beginning, Brownie and I settled down to conventional raises of two bits (a quarter). We had the bidding to ourselves, and the auctioneer had it easy. He merely looked from one of us to the other after each two-bit raise. As we neared the six-dollar point, I became aware that a small urchin named Orville was standing in the aisle at the end of the row in which I sat, trying to get my attention. I waved him away impatiently and went on bidding, wincing inwardly at each potential inroad into my pitifully small capital and the vanishing coat reserve. Orville finally muttered, "Here, you goof," and passed a folded piece of paper along the row of people to me.

Intent on the contest, I didn't even look at it. When Brownie bid "Six seventy-five," I tried a last desperate measure. Strongly, I called out, "Eight dollars!" and tried to make the words sound as if it were now time to stop the chicken-feed business and get down to some real, sure-enough bidding. The maneuver didn't work. Brownie, not to be fooled, or stampeded into recklessness either, said calmly, "Eight twenty-five," thus topping my entire pocket content by two bits.

Mr. Toomis waited. Nothing came from my side, of course. I had shot my wad, and it would have been gross misconduct to bid more than you could pay in cash when you claimed the prize. There was no such thing as "charging" at a box supper as we did at the stores. Mr. Toomis tried a spiel:

"I am bid eight twenty-five for this magnificent repast. Do I hear eight fifty? Surely it is worth that trifling sum merely to gnaw a gizzard in the company of the charming little lady who prepared this splendidly decorated box."

Trifling sum indeed! My life's blood. Four bits more than my summer's savings. . . . When I still didn't speak out, he knew I was sunk and went into what was for me the final dirge: "Eight twenty-five once . . ." and so on to the bitter end. Brownie not only had bested me but had good reason to believe that he had won for Marilee the very great prestige of having drawn the highest bid of the evening, the ultimate triumph at a box supper and an honor coveted by all the single girls.

I got a small gloating consolation from seeing Brownie, on the way to claim his prize, stop beside his father and uneasily whisper something to him. His dad brought out his pocket-book with a look that said plainly, "I'll see you later about this bit of foolishness, young man." A few people snickered, comprehending from this by-play that Brownie had overshot his personal resources.

Low in my seat and lower in spirit, I looked at the paper little Orville had brought. It was a note. I read:

Dear Marion:

Belle has copied my box exactly and tipped off her Uncle Albert to put it up before mine to fool Brownie. I took the bachelor's-button spray off my box, and that's how you can tell it from Belle's.

Marilee

I had to read it three times before its meaning dawned with an overwhelming impact of exultation. Brownie, that hound, was stuck with Belle, and my incomparable Marilee was still free, her box unsold. Moreover, she had tried her best to warn me of the situation before it was too late. I knew then that the poets spoke truly when they told of singing hearts.

Almost immediately, Marilee's box came up for auction; it was square, it was green, it had a red ribbon—and no flower spray of bachelor's-buttons.

As the auctioneer began his harangue, I turned around and said harshly to my sister, "Give me that four bits you have." I knew she had fifty cents, because I had seen Grandpa give it to her that day for some purpose and I also knew she hadn't had a chance to spend it.

My tone was so implacable that she didn't argue before handing over the half dollar. She knew anyway that under the circumstances I would repay the money no matter what sacrifice might be required of me to do so. With the coin she gave me a wide-eyed but, I like to think, sympathetic look. . . . I turned back to face the auctioneer as he asked for an opening bid on the box in hand.

"EIGHT FIFTY!" I said explosively.

A murmur ran through the audience, because it was clear that for some special reason I was determined that the owner of this particular box should have the high-bid distinction of the evening. Hence the startling first bid, so outrageously high as to discourage any further bidding.

Mr. Toomis, with a sort of bemused curiosity, examined again the box poised on the upstretched fingers of his left hand. He must have noticed its similarity to the one described to him earlier by his niece, Belle. He smiled faintly, nodded to himself, and brought down his gavel with a louder bang than usual.

"Sold for eight fifty!" he said with finality.

Brownie and Belle must have enjoyed the repast they shared as a result of the mix-up that evening, because they began going steady afterward. I am sure they had many a laugh, chiefly at my expense, over that box supper.

I never did tell Grandpa of my piece of foolishness, because I was in no mood that shivery winter to listen to a little sermonette from him about impulsive gestures inspired by vanity and romantic notions. He failed to notice that I had no topcoat. Grandma observed and no doubt worried some but asked no questions. Sis kept quiet and in due time got back her half dollar.

As for my budding romance with Marilee, it never quite flowered. It withered a little every time I looked at her, causing her more puzzlement than concern, since she was innocently unaware of the reason for my diminishing ardor. But it was a curious fact that the sight of her brought to my mouth a thick, tweedy sort of taste, suggestive of the topcoat I didn't have. And my distaste for fried chicken, already strong, increased every time I thought of the *pièce de résistance* in the box that brought to Marilee the coveted high-bid distinction of the evening. I am sure we both remember that box supper, but for quite different reasons.

# XX

I ran away from home only once.

It happened in the summer of 1917, a few months after the United States entered World War I, and it was unpremeditated.

A large army installation, Camp Beauregard, was being built at Alexandria in central Louisiana, and there was a great deal of extravagant talk about the high wages being paid to carpenters and other skilled labor for work on the barracks and other structures. Nearly every undrafted man in town who knew the difference between a spirit level and a handsaw and had little to hold him back headed for Alexandria and prosperity. Word came back that it was all true that carpenters and masons and even unskilled workers were being paid from five dollars a day to a dollar an hour. Other men departed, even a few farmers who decided it was worthwhile abandoning their crops.

None of this excitement was for me and my friends to enjoy. I was fourteen, too young for military service, too small and inept with tools to work at a building trade. One sixteen-year-old in our group, Duvall Stallings, got into the army by saying he was eighteen and eventually went overseas with the American Expeditionary Forces. The rest of us felt left out of things and moped about it.

I knew Grandpa had fought in what Southerners call the War Between the States, and I asked him about it. According to my transcribed schoolboy notes, his response went like this:

"I must have been the only private in the Confederate Army, if you believe the stories told by other veterans, none of whom will admit to a rank lower than captain. I missed most of the fighting and was in only one real shooting skirmish. I hurt no one and no one hurt me, but I won a citation of which I am right proud. History shows that the eleven states of the Confederacy fought a needless war for the wrong reasons; and it is well that we lost, but in the short time I was in the fighting there was an enemy confronting us on a battlefield and I felt it was my duty to fight him, regardless of which side was right.

"My company lay one day behind some earth breastworks, and since the Yankees were shooting in our direction from a few hundred feet, maybe yards away, I reared up between their volleys and shot back. My company commander cited me as follows: 'Blackman, you son of a bitch, lie down there!'

"That's the way it's going to be all of your life, Son; every time you do something you believe to be right, someone above you, beside you, or below you is sure to call you a son of a bitch. But don't let that stop you; just fight when and how you can, so long as you believe you are right and no longer. . . . It's a wonder I didn't have to face a court-martial for insubordination, because I didn't lie down and I kept shooting. I guess I'm just a natural-born Rebel. Some say I'm just plain mulish, but I don't consider that to be an insult. A mule is only a smart hybrid; responds to a carrot quicker than to a stick. . . . Did I ever tell you I was born in New York State? Just a damyankee, transplanted young."

One idle summer day of restlessness three of us hopped a northbound freight for the up-down-up ride to Riverton, Kelly, and back to Grayson. On the southbound leg of our stolen ride we were talking enviously about Camp Beauregard and Owen said,

"You know, I hear they are paying water boys on the construction job down there fifty cents an hour."

John and I looked at him. "What all does a water boy have to do?" I asked.

"He just fills a water bucket at a well somewhere and carries it around where the men are working. When somebody wants a drink he hands him a dipper and holds the bucket while he helps himself," Owen explained.

"And for that he gets fifty cents an hour? If he worked ten hours, that would be five dollars a day."

"Anybody could do that."

"We could do that."

We all said at once, "Let's do it."

So we rode through Kelly, past Olla and Rochelle and Georgetown and the other little towns on to Alexandria—a ride that lasted sixty-five miles and about four hours. It was dark when we jumped off the train in the yards at the edge of town (to escape the unwelcome attentions of the railroad's special police) and walked the rest of the way—

The rest of the way to what?

We thought of that for the first time. Several other problems occurred to us for the first time. Where were we going to stay? Eat? With what? We took stock: I had fifteen cents, each of them had a quarter. Naturally we were hungry; we had been on freight trains most of the day with nothing to eat. I forget what they bought for food; I got three bananas with my three nickels, but I saved two for the next day.

We wandered around the streets for a couple of hours and finally crept into a dark church. Three pews served as couches, hard but at least sheltered . . . It was a long night.

The next morning we ate half of our meager rations and inquired the way to the camp a few miles outside the city limits. Before eight o'clock there were wagonloads of all sorts of material going that way and we soon hitched a ride.

The sprawling campsite appeared to be a scene of utter confusion with row after row of frame structures on brick foundations in various stages of construction, but I suppose it actually was orderly. We were fascinated and wandered around most of the day just looking and trying to keep out of the way of the workers with their saws, hammers, T-squares, levels, trowels, and other tools. But we did not forget what we were there for and kept an eye open for someone in authority, a boss, a foreman, or somebody who might be an employer.

Finally, we picked out a man who seemed to be directing a crew of men, so Owen walked boldly up to him and asked, "Mister, do you need some more water boys?"

The man looked curiously at him and at us. "Water boys?" he asked. "What for?"

"Why, uh, why—" Owen stuttered, "to take drinking water around to the men at work."

"This ain't a desert, Son," the man said. "There are miles of water pipes under this place and a hydrant about every fifty feet. Man wants a drink of water, he helps hisself."

"Oh," Owen said inadequately.

"Where you boys live?"

"Grayson."

"Where's that?"

"It's upstate in Caldwell Parish."

"Bet your folks don't know where you are."

We had begun to think about that, too, a bit uneasily. Nobody said anything.

"You better get back home," the man advised, "before you get hurt or into trouble."

We were about to reach that conclusion ourselves, so we picked out way through the disorder and started back to town.

"You and your fifty cents an hour," I said scornfully to Owen.

"It's not my fault," he protested. "I heard some men talking and that's exactly what they said. I didn't just make it up."

"I bet they had never been near Camp Beauregard," John said. "Or else they were pulling somebody's leg."

"Not mine," Owen said. "They didn't even know I was listening."

"I'm going home," I said. "I'm hungry."

"Me, too."

"Me, too."

It was dark by the time we got back to town—we had to walk—and we didn't fancy a four-hour night ride on a slow freight, so we went back to the church to spend the night. I ate my last banana and Owen and John finished whatever it was they had bought. The pangs of hunger were eased a little but they soon were stronger than ever. It is incredible how famished a fourteen-year-old boy can get. . . . It was another long night.

Some time past midmorning we managed to climb unobserved into an empty gondola car in a string of boxcars that was being pulled out of the railroad yards on the north edge of Alexandria. . . . The ride seemed as long as the night had been, but it actually was shorter than the trip down had been. There were no more than twenty cars in the string and they appeared to be empties. The locomotive barreled them along almost like a passenger train, even on the upgrades.

I was the first to realize what we were in for, and my heart seemed to sink into my empty stomach.

"We'll be going like a bat out of hell through Grayson," I said. "We won't dare hop off. Break our fool necks."

Sure enough, we sped upgrade through Grayson at a speed of at least twenty miles an hour. I peered longingly over the side of the gondola as we went past our house. No one was in sight. I tightened my belt another notch.

"It'll slow down enough at the river bridge in Columbia to let us get off," John predicted. "We won't have to go on to Riverton."

"How we gonna get back from Columbia?" Owen wondered.

"Walk," I said grimly. "I'm sick of freights."

We got off at the bridge all right and we walked back to Grayson. That is, they walked; I strode. I lengthened my steps until I was outdistancing them, and I soon pulled ahead.

"Look at him go," they jeered. "Must be the first time he's ever been away from home without his folks."

I was soon out of hearing, then out of sight around a bend. I still had my Ingersoll watch, and I noted that I walked the five miles in less than an hour. It was midafternoon when I looked down the high road and saw my pin oak tree. The front lawn that year had grown a thick cover of bitter weeds, and their blossoms made a sea of yellow around the tree.

I thought I had never seen a lovelier sight.

No one was in view when I entered the house and headed straight for the dining room, but I heard sounds from the kitchen as I opened the old safe, as the food cabinet was called. We had no ice box then.

There was a long deep dish on the bottom shelf half full of black-eyed peas. They were cold of course, with a thin film of grease on top, but I snatched up a spoon and began shoveling peas from the dish into my mouth.

I hadn't believed anything could taste so delicious.

As I was gulping down the last mouthful, Grandpa sauntered in from the kitchen, carrying a steaming and aromatic cup.

"Coffee time," he said. "Here's yours." He looked at the empty dish. "I get the impression you're glad to be back."

"I sure am," I said fervently.

"I also suspect you're back to stay."

"You bet I am."

"That's good," Grandpa said, nodding his head approvingly. "Tell me all about it some time, if you like."

"I'll tell you now," I said.

I told him and I was sure he understood. About all he said though was, "You could have slept in worse places than a church."

# XXI

Grandpa seemed to have an ambivalent attitude toward churches and organized religion. He encouraged me to attend Sunday school, and I did so regularly, but it was more of a social event than a religious rite, and Grayson's community activities were rather limited. I noticed that while Grandma nearly always attended the church service that followed Sunday school, Grandpa never did. After I remained a few times for the service, I thought I knew why; I was not impressed by the sermons to which I only half listened. The preachers

of that time and place were either droning bores or belonged
to the hell-and-damnation school. It seemed to me that if they
were unable to arouse a positive interest in heaven it was a
sorry substitute to try to frighten me with lurid descriptions
of the dreadful punishments awaiting sinners in hell.

In time I learned Grandpa was scornful not necessarily of
the brand of preaching but of the attitude of the community
toward the formal practices of religion; he regarded it as
hypocritical and divisive, having little to do with his own
strong religious beliefs.

When we first moved to Grayson, the only church in town
was that of the M.P. denomination (Methodist Protestant),
but members of the other two major denominations worshiped in it. The ministers took turns at preaching and con-
ducting revival meetings (protracted meetings) that lasted
from one to three weeks with nightly services. It was the
equivalent of the modern Community Church.

But after a few years, the members of the second Methodist
branch decided they wanted their own edifice. They raised
the money, built the M.E. Church (Methodist Episcopal) and
installed their own underpaid minister. Then the Baptists got
restless and independent, and the third church was erected to
compete with the other two in a village with a population too
small to fill even one regularly.

It was then that Grandpa, who had joined the Baptist
Church in Manifest because it was the only one available
there, became disgusted and stopped attending any church at
all. He never set foot in the Grayson church of his own
denomination.

"Hypocrites all," he scoffed. "They all pretend to be
worshiping the same God, so what difference does it make
what denomination builds the church?"

I continued to attend Sunday school in the M.P. Church,

but I sometimes went to prayer meetings in another church, depending upon which girls in town were expected to be there.

Grandpa firmly believed in God and having been a farmer close to nature all of his life he worshiped at his own shrines: dawn, with its sun-and-cloud-streaked grandeur; the recurrent miracle of dew or frost on grass; and all things that grew green and fruitful. He called these wonders works of God, more real than man-made edifices and altars, and if he felt in need of prayers he offered them when he was contemplating such manifestations of creation.

"There has to be a Supreme Intelligence, call Him what you will," he often told me. "There just must be a pattern and a reason underlying this wonderful and inexplicable universe. Its very existence demands a belief in a Force that has to be divine, or at least superhuman if you prefer that term."

When I began to ask questions about the logic of his belief in a Deity, he said, "You must go to the authorities." He first persuaded me to read in its entirety his copy of the 1611 King James Version of the Bible, quite an undertaking for a youth in his teens accustomed only to Sunday school skipping about in the Scriptures. I found it rewarding reading just for the sound effects, since the King James abounds in sonorous sentences that can be rolled off the tongue and savored like organ music.

Even then I was almost as infatuated with the sound as with the meaning of words and I was particularly delighted by such vivid picture lines as the one from Solomon's Song in the Old Testament: "Stay me with flagons, comfort me with apples: for I am sick of love." I read that one aloud to Grandpa.

"Grand, isn't it," he said.

"But just what does it mean?" I asked.

"Those are figures of speech," he said; "they mean just about what you want them to mean."

Symbolism or whatever, they conjured up for me all sorts of exciting pictures, provoking endless speculation, none of which contributed to nor detracted from a belief in God.

Years later I was outraged when I came upon a monstrosity called the Revised Standard Version of the American Standard Version, published in 1901, and looked up my favorite quotation. I found it in a chapter now called Song of Solomon instead of the simpler Solomon's Song, and it read: "*Sustain* me with *raisins, refresh* me with apples; for I am sick *with* love." How awful!

When I had finished reading the Bible, I reported to Grandpa that I had found the language entrancing; the repetitions in the various Books by the Apostles monotonous; and the doctrine unconvincing.

"The Bible offers only one form of religion," he said. "You may as well learn about some others, since the majority of the people in the world follow one or another of them."

From the shelf holding all that remained of his collection of books he took down a volume I had looked at but passed up. It was written by a then well-known theologian and it described the various non-Christian religions and forms of paganism in India, China, elsewhere in the Orient, and Africa. I read all of it too; some of it was hard going but I got the ideas.

"They all have one thing in common," I said, "a belief in the existence of a Deity. But in none of them is there any proof."

"Proof, no," Grandpa conceded. "Nobody has any proof in the sense you mean. But I and millions of others have faith that is proof enough for us. Sometimes simple belief has to suffice. This newfangled thing called radio is absolutely im-

possible to exist when you consider it logically. It is not
believable.

"But it exists," he went on earnestly. "Music and words
are sent out through the air on something called waves; they
go around corners, through brick walls and other solid obstacles; and they come out of crystal set earphones with just
the same original sound. I'll never understand radio or the
principles on which it works, but I have faith in its existence
because I can see or hear, rather, its manifestations."

"Aha!" I said. (I thought I had him there.) "I can't explain
it either, but there are scientists who can. You can't compare
an Apostle or a preacher with a scientist. Nobody can prove
the existence of a God nor explain Him, or how or by whom
*He* was created."

Although I had been reading about forms of deism, I hadn't
paid much attention to the terms used for dissenters. Grandpa
provided some definitions.

"You don't contend there is no God?" he asked.

"No, of course not."

"Then you are not an atheist. An atheist is one who says
flatly there is no God or any other kind of Supreme Being."

"No, I'm not that," I agreed, "because it doesn't stand to
reason. An atheist can't *know* one way or the other anything
I don't know—how can he say for sure there is or isn't? I
just admit that I don't know whether He does or doesn't
exist."

"Then that makes you what we call an agnostic," he explained, "neither a believer nor a disbeliever. As for me, I
believe in a Supreme Being, but what I don't believe is that
there is any real difference among creeds and denominations."

"Are you an infidel because you don't go to any of the
churches?" I asked.

"No, no," he said. "A man who is a nonbeliever in a given

religion, such as Christianity, is called an infidel by the be-
lievers. I believe in Christ as well as God, so I am a Christian
—I don't *know* there is a Christ, but I have faith that He
exists. There are others who believe in God but not in his
Son, such as the Jews. So they can't be Christians, but that
doesn't mean they are not religious or that they are wrong,
although some bigots would say that is so.

"Oh, well," he concluded, "it's your problem. Maybe I
should warn you though before we drop the subject that the
time is certain to come—that's my belief—when you will
learn the final truth. I only hope it won't be too late; I can't
believe it will ever be too late."

He never brought up the subject again, nor did I.

# XXII

It was easy to get my grandfather to discourse freely on any subject except the unfortunate career of my father. He told me briefly that he was a brilliant man and an excellent doctor but had lost two medical practices because of his drinking. Six months before his second child was to be born he drove his rig to the railroad station in Mansfield, hitched the horse to a post, and boarded a train for Texas. He never came back. My mother waited for him as long as she could, then went back to her family in Plain Dealing.

"And nobody ever heard from him or of him again?" I asked Grandpa.

"Never again," Grandpa said matter-of-factly. He was not bitter nor harsh in his judgment; he merely was sad.

"Don't let it worry you," he said reassuringly. "It's possible to inherit a weak trait of character, but I doubt that anyone ever inherited a thirst for strong drink. If so, it ought to work the other way, too. I've never even tasted liquor, so why didn't he inherit my nonthirst?"

"Did you feel somehow guilty or responsible?" I asked curiously. "Is that why you took us—his children—to live with you?"

"I don't believe I ever gave that angle a single thought," he said after reflecting a moment. "Somebody had to do it, and we were in the best position to take on the job. All our children were grown, educated, and married, and we weren't exactly destitute."

"But Grandpa," I objected, "that meant starting all over at nearly sixty with a second family after you had spent nearly half your life raising the first one. Hardly seems fair."

"Oh well," he said, smiling kindly. "It hasn't been too bad. In fact, it's been sort of interesting. Just you see to it," he warned with mock sternness, "that we aren't wasting our time."

It was plain to me that he did not care to say any more on the subject, so I asked my gentle grandmother if she could add anything that might shed some light on the behavior of John Cyrenus Blackman, who was her second son and the fourth of seven children she had helped to rear.

"I'm sure your grandfather told you all I know about what happened to your father," she said softly, "but I can tell you this about your mother: She loved him, and did not stop loving him when he went away."

She went to a bureau, rummaged in a drawer, and returned with a faded letter envelope addressed with an indelible pencil to Mrs. M. C. Blackman, Manifest, La. She handed it to me.

"Her last letter is inside. Put it away and keep it," she suggested. "It will tell you truly that she loved him." She paused a moment, then added gently, "I loved him too; more than all the rest, I'm afraid."

In my room I looked at the Plain Dealing postmark and calculated that the date was just thirty-three days (leap year) before my sister was born on March 6, 1904, and my mother died. I was sixteen months old. The letter, written a day earlier on narrow ruled paper, addressed my grandmother as "My Dear Mother" and referred to several of my father's brothers, sisters, and in-laws. I read:

Will now attempt to write you a few lines, but I can hardly see as I have a sty on my eye. I expect you will be at Effie's when this letter reaches Manifest. Am sorry you did not come up here, for Son and I would like very much to see you.

Dink came home Thursday and was glad to get here. She was so tired of school and begged so hard to come, so we knew she would be needed and is good help anyway. Sometimes she helps me so much with Son, carries him upstairs and down for me, helps take wood and water, which is certainly a great help, for these stairs nearly tire me out sometimes.

I am so homesick I am nearly crazy, though I haven't any home of my own. Sometimes I believe I will go crazy. It just seems as if I cannot bear my troubles. No one on earth can know what I suffer, but I try to bear it the best I can, for I know it is best not to give way.

It is a great blessing my child was given me, for no telling where I would be tonight if it were not for him. My life would be ruined, but I love my darling baby, and am so thankful God has spared his little life to me, for he is all I have. But, Mother, when I think I will never see old Cy's face again, it nearly breaks my heart for, oh, I love him.

If he could only be with me when I get sick, for he was so good to me before. But I find everything different to what it used to be. There is no place like home, however simple it may be.

Well, Mother, do you ever hear from Clara? It seems as if she never gets any of my letters. I cannot understand why all of them are lost. Milton came to see me Sunday. He looks well. Birdie and baby were down this eve. Baby is awfully sweet. She is learning to talk now and Doctor is the happiest man anywhere.

I do wish you and Father could see Son now. He certainly is cute, full of mischief, but is so smart. Has a terrible cough and cold. Keeps me uneasy about him, for this weather is so changeable. I am afraid he will have grippe. I am just as careful as can be. I guess Fannie and her babes are getting along all right. Do wish I could see everybody, anyway.

Well, Mother, as my eye hurts me, will close with much love to all. Write real soon, for I do enjoy your letters. Son sends Grandma and Grandpa lots of kisses. He waits on me real good, brings different things to me, and today he saw me bring in some stove wood, so he brings in a stick by his little self. Oh! He is Mama's little man.

Bye bye.

Lovingly,
Maude

My first thought when I finished reading this poignant little missive was that my grandmother must have felt even sadder than my grandfather about their errant son and his grieving wife. My second thought was that I should share their sadness, but I couldn't. I was touched, but in an impersonal way. I just didn't feel that anything had happened to me. I had never felt a lack of parents.

# XXIII

---

My family and friends who are aware of my marked aversion to manual labor or even any exercise more strenuous than strolling are inclined to be skeptical of my claimed former prowess at plowing, gardening, milking, chopping and picking cotton, and similar farm pursuits. Eyebrows are lifted too when I casually mention that I was one of two forwards on the basketball team in all of my four years in Grayson Agricultural High School and captain for two of them. But it is true.

Basketball was the sole team sport at the school in my time there, about a quarter of a century after Dr. James E. Naismith invented the game. It was played from the day school opened each year until the eight-month term ended. Although the school enrollment exceeded the village population, there weren't enough boys in the upper grades to field twenty-two players to make up first and second football teams for scrimmaging in practice for matches with other school teams.

Another factor was that a football cost seven or eight dollars while a basketball could be obtained in Monroe for about three and a half dollars. A committee of one faculty member and two seniors was appointed before school opened each year to raise the basketball money. There were only three merchants in town who could be counted on to contribute and they balked at any sum over a dollar. The coach kicked in the other fifty cents.

On the first day of school the ball was blown up with a bicycle pump, and the long season was on. There was competition between the first and second teams at Grayson High every single school day, at both morning and afternoon twenty-minute recesses and half of the noon dinner hour.

The coach was called Mr. Jay because he signed his name J. J. McKeithen, and no one knew what the initials stood for. He became the principal of Grayson High the year I went upstairs to the eighth grade in 1916. At the beginning of that school term a charming young woman named DeEtte Eglin came to Grayson from Alexandria to take the post of home economics teacher. Mr. Jay began a courtship of Miss DeEtte and married her in the summer of 1917. Their first child was born on May 28, 1918, and christened John Julian. He was mistakenly (as it turned out) referred to thereafter as Junior, because his initials were the same as his father's. He was still called that by his parents and their neighbors after he was elected Governor of Louisiana in 1960 to begin his first four-year term in 1961.

Mr. Jay was a dedicated school principal and was the type of man to whom Grandpa would lend money without security. I don't believe he knew anything about basketball except the rules, but he believed in organized sport and in Grayson that meant basketball. There was no one on the faculty qualified to serve as coach so he volunteered; he continued in the dual role of principal and athletic director until he resigned a month and twenty-one days before I got my diploma.

One year Mr. Jay did put together a track team of sorts, but the most promising competitors were a couple of hundred-yard dash runners: John Carroll, who learned from some source the orthodox stride; and Duvall Stallings (pronounced with a short *a*), who ran blind with his head thrown back and his chin pointing upward into the wind at a forty-five-degree angle. They usually finished in a dead heat, but not fast enough to place in meets with other high schools in the parish. I could be counted on for third place and one point in the pole vault event, since the twelve-foot pole was the equalizer for my stature of five-feet-four or -five, and I had only 110 pounds to hoist over the bar. (I have since added a few inches and pounds.) But a one-point score wins no track meets and the venture into that field was not repeated.

That was about it in athletics at Grayson High, except that in my freshman year I was one of several who were awarded bronze medals by the New Orleans *Times-Picayune* (my practice paper for home study of journalism) for chinning themselves on a horizontal bar fourteen times. That seemed a strange sort of event and an arbitrary number of chinnings for a statewide paper to sponsor. All in all, I undoubtedly was the worst all-around high school athlete in competition in the State of Louisiana with the title of team captain.

One may wonder then how it came about that even allowing for Grayson High's paucity of material I was a member of the varsity basketball team for four years and skipper in my junior and senior years. The explanation is that I became a student of topography and mastered after school hours the art of smooth basketball dribbling over ravine-rough terrain.

The school had no gymnasium, so the ninety-by-forty-foot court was laid out on the gentle campus slope where it leveled off a bit on the west side, but not enough to prevent the rectangle from slanting at an angle like a shuffleboard area on the deck of a ship rolling in a medium-rough sea—except that it always remained this-way and never went that-way. As a result, every time there was a Louisiana downpour freshets of rain water seeking its own level coursed across the bare redland earth of the court, leaving meandering ditches up to six inches deep, especially on the lower side. Trying out for the position of forward, I practiced dribbling across these obstacles whenever I could find the time. I learned to vary the rhythm of the bouncing advance toward either goal so as to hit smooth ground with a long or a short stride on both sides on the rivulet ravines. . . . Passing to a teammate on our quintet was a last resort in an emergency, such as being surrounded by all five of the opposing players. We were all individualists; usually it was every man for himself, and good dribbling was a skill more highly regarded than accurate passing.

The first team's winning strategy as we developed it was a lot less complex than a Clausewitz military campaign, with me as the pivotal member of the attack. None of us was tall by latter-day standards. Our varsity center until he was graduated a year ahead of me was Owen Jones, who was only five-feet-ten. He won his position because he could spring four feet into the air from a standing, flat-footed stance. Thus he could top the best reach of the second-string center, who was an even six feet but rather earthbound. I always hovered near center when the ball was tossed for the jump, and Owen's instructions were to bat the ball to me if he could or to a teammate who would pass it to me pronto. Then I would be off like a flash on a ditch-hopping dribble to the backboard with its netless hoop for a goal. If I was lucky in evading my guard, I could make two passes at the basket, one from in front and one upon recovery of the rebounding ball while I was whooshing past the backboard post.

Mr. Jay had to function as referee as well as coach, but his activities in the first capacity usually were limited to tossing up the ball between the centers at the beginning of each half and after each field or foul goal, blowing a tin whistle, and retreating to safety on a sideline.

The ball was called out-of-bounds if it went wild out of the approximated rectangle on a pass or when a player stepped on a telltale gum tree ball or thistle, indicating he had gone over a more or less imaginary and elastic boundary line unmarked by slaked lime. Mr. Jay then blew a blast and the ball went to the out-of-bounds player's opposite number, who stood in the rough and tossed it back into play.

The only fouls Mr. Jay ever called were for flagrant holding or something known as the double dribble. No personal fouls were ever called for body contacts unless a player was practically maimed.

I had plenty of painful body contacts with one of my second-team guards named Joe Henley. He was a maternal uncle of my good friend Henley Biggs and lived with Dr. and Mrs. Biggs for some time while going to school with his nephew, who was a year or two younger. Joe Henley was a tall, skinny fellow who seemed to me to be all elbows, knees, and other hard bones which he simply interposed in my path toward the goal with a great deal of flailing action. I bore ominous-looking bruises all over my body from late September to early May; for these Mr. Jay had sympathy but no preventive measures or curative ointments. Personal fouls for body contacts? Nonsense. Nothing personal was intended when Henley's Uncle Joe inflicted a bruise; he was unfailingly good-humored when he was trying his best to cripple me.

It seemed to me that Mr. Jay's only coaching of the varsity was to yell "Pass it to Marion!" And his shouted coaching of the second team was the warning, "Can't you see Marion is unguarded?" But I suppose it was natural for every player to think of team activities in terms of his part in them.

However, my topographic dribbling technique did contribute something to the strategy that enabled us to win nearly all our home games. And since we always pleaded our very real poverty in travel money, we persuaded opponents to come to Grayson from as far away as Monroe and Ruston, and on our ravine-ravaged court we piled up a respectable record of victories. Our visiting teams just couldn't cope with our unfamiliar ball court canyonettes.

Thus it came about that in my junior year we became ambitious enough to enter the state's first high school basketball tournament. How we raised the money to pay for six round-trip tickets to Baton Rouge 'way down South I can't recall, but I'm sure Mr. Jay was in there pitching with some sort of financial wizardry. What's more, we somehow acquired real uniforms instead of the usual makeshift old short pants.

Sad to relate, the tournament was an unmitigated disaster for the Grayson team; we were humiliatingly eliminated in the first-round game with Coushatta. Even worse, in losing we got our hands on the ball just once—and that was on an out-of-bounds call.

Such a poor performance was hard to believe, but there were several unusual and unfamiliar circumstances. For one thing, the court had a grass cover instead of being the bare clay we were accustomed to, and there were no ravines for me to dribble over expertly while confusing the opposing team. The ball itself was new and still completely round, unlike the slightly elliptical one ours always became after the first couple of months of hard play. This might have thrown us off our stride—if we had been able to get our hands on the ball—and it probably confused us some anyway.

The real explanation though was the fact that the Coushatta coach, unlike Mr. Jay, had attended a university that had a first-class basketball team and a coach who had taught him as a player some tricks; or as it seemed to us a system that worked like magic.

The Coushatta center was not only taller but a jumper to equal our Owen Jones. When the ball was tossed up between them he took prompt and complete directional charge; and his teammates deployed into an intricate but smoothly functioning pattern. The ball went phhttt! phhtttt! from one player to another, crisscross, and down the field, and then into the basket for a goal.

When we finally got the ball on an out-of-bounds call, one of our guards put it back into play; a Coushatta guard intercepted it, and there went another two-point goal to add into a final score of something like ninety-eight to zero.

The secret was that the Coushatta team, like most others since 1891 I am sure, had a set of signals for effective teamwork offensives. (It needed no defensive plays or signals against us.) Mr. Jay and the opposing team coaches we had encountered in our matches in north-central Louisiana had never, to my knowledge, practiced such trickery as play signals.

We had never heard of such. We just played the game by dribble and by ear.

# XXIV

---

My high school career and life in Grayson ended on a sour note, but Grandpa Blackman responded characteristically to it.

When I decided, rightly or wrongly, at the age of thirteen that the best way to become a newspaperman was to study journalism at the state university, I realized that money would be the greatest obstacle.

I learned that I wouldn't need much. Lodging in the Pentagon barracks at what was called then "The Ole War Skule" was free, as was tuition, to residents of the state. All male freshmen and sophomores were required to become members of the Reserve Officers Training Corps and to wear at all times uniforms that were bought cheaply through the university under a contract let in competitive bidding. In the junior and senior years, R.O.T.C. was optional, and the student members usually wore civvies except when drilling. (I could worry about that when the time came.) I was sure I could get a job waiting on tables to earn my own meals; every fraternity house had such student help drawn from the ranks of non-Greeks, called "Barbarians."

The biggest cash outlay would be about $150 a year for textbooks, laboratory fees, and kindred incidental expenses. Fortunately, a four-year $600 scholarship was being offered at that time for just that purpose by some Pelican State philanthropist long since forgotten. The scholarship was to be awarded to the valedictorian of each graduating class in all of the state's high schools, and the requirements for that honor were to be set by the school principal. That was my aim for the class of 1920.

To qualify under the Grayson custom for the class position of valedictorian and the cash award, I had to score the highest average grades in the class of 1920 during four years of high school; and with very little competition from the uninterested majority of my fellow students I did so. My grades up to graduation week were a bit higher in all subjects than the 95 percent that automatically, under a school rule, exempted me from taking any final examinations. I had never taken a final exam in high school.

At this point, another factor affected the windup of my senior year. The village fathers had connived with the school authorities to put into effect an eight o'clock curfew on week nights for students, with the laudable purpose of inducing them to do their homework instead of carousing over ice-cream sodas and Cokes at Biggs Drugstore until its 10 P.M. closing time.

Mr. Jay McKeithen had resigned as principal on the first day of April that year to go into the business of buying and selling timber, the better to support Miss DeEtte and Junior. He was succeeded as principal by a spinster member of the high school faculty, a dedicated teacher and a stern disciplinarian.

I didn't consult her or anyone else in a position to rule on the curfew question, as I probably should have done, but I reasoned with what seemed to me sound logic that since I had no home studying to do for examinations I was not required to take in my last week of school, the curfew rule was not applicable to me. If exempt from exams, why not exempt from curfew imposed to encourage study?

So I went calling upon my current girl friend on a Wednesday night in May of 1920. I long remembered the date.

The girl was Mary Alice, a member of the family across the railroad from our house that owned one of the two private libraries in the village. She was a year my senior and had been graduated from high school the previous year. Our romance was not a very torrid one, but she found little to do in Grayson, and I was welcome to call upon her that night.

To enliven the evening, she whipped up a batch of cane syrup and other ingredients into the confection called taffy. I wasn't particularly fond of this sticky delight, since I had been eating sugar cane syrup at all meals ever since I could remember, but I went along with the refreshment suggestion. When the cooked stuff showed signs of solidifying, we shifted the romantic scene from the kitchen to the living room. There, we buttered our hands, took stances a foot or so apart and brazenly engaged in a parlor recreation known as a taffy pull, right in front of an unshaded window overlooking a street leading to the Baptist church. We were so lost to decency we didn't care who saw us. Our pulling back and forth of the still ductile mixture was supposed to refine its texture, make it creamier in color, and more easily chipped into bite-sized chunks. At least, that's the way I recall the purpose and technique of the taffy pull.

Wednesday was prayer meeting night at the churches, and shortly after eight o'clock the spinster principal of the high school passed my girl's home on her way to obtain some probably sorely needed divine guidance. She looked into the open window in passing and caught me red-handed (butter-yellow-handed, to be more exact) in a violation of the letter if not the spirit of the curfew law.

The next morning, this paragon of virtuous discipline exposed me to obloquy before the entire student body in a general assembly in the auditorium as a senior setting a shamelessly bad example by flouting the law. She then pronounced judgment and fixed punishment to fit the crime: There would be no valedictorian that year and no scholarship to the university from the graduating class of 1920.

I was too stubborn or too proud or too indignant to plead with her on my own behalf, but I thought of my quiet, shy, studious classmate, Norma Fisher, and put in a word for her after the general assembly. She had finished second in the competition for valedictorian; I knew she could use the scholarship because she was the only other member of the senior class who had evinced any special interest in a higher education and her financial prospects were even bleaker than mine.

"Why not give the kudos and the cash to Norma?" I asked

the principal. "Her four-year average was only a couple of points below mine; she isn't as adept at memorizing dull subjects as I am. I see no reason why the scholarship should go to waste just because I blew it. After all, you have the privilege of choosing anyone you please as valedictorian, regardless of grades."

The principal was adamant and, by her own lights, fair. I had earned the honor in accordance with the rules that had always been followed, but had forfeited it by my defiant disobedience. Norma had not earned it, according to those same standards, so she was not entitled to it, deserving as she might be otherwise. So—no valedictorian and no scholarship in Grayson High in 1920. Selah!

Naturally, I was despondent over the loss of the needed cash award after I had done a lot of disagreeable studying to earn it, but what probably made the principal's ex cathedra sentence harder to bear was a wound to my ego. I had already written and practiced delivery of a splendid valedictory address—my maiden public speech, now never to be spoken.

Graduation night, usually a memorable occasion for high school seniors, was a complete bust as far as I was concerned . . . and taffy joined fried chicken on my blacklist of edibles.

I told Grandpa all about it, of course. He wasted no sympathy on me.

"A rule is a rule," he said tartly. "If you don't like it, you try to change it, but you obey it while it's in effect. I happen to think this rule is not fair or even logical, so I'm going to see what can be done to amend it."

And he proceeded forthwith to do so. He exerted pressure on the chairman of the school board (probably by waving a demand promissory note under his nose) to call a special session. Then Grandpa put on his fading wedding finery and went off to attend the meeting. He returned beaming with satisfaction and self-esteem.

"The rule has been changed," he reported. "It's too late to do you any good, but you will have successors. Hereafter, any student whose grades exempt him from taking the final examinations will not be required to observe the eight o'clock curfew during examination week."

A small triumph, perhaps, but it concluded my growing-up period in Grayson on a note that I decided was not so sour after all.

When I went away soon afterward to follow another path to higher education, I carried with me a mental picture that never dimmed: Grandpa Blackman, bedecked in outdated toggery like a country dandy of the 1860's, going off to do battle for something he thought was right for someone else, and returning victorious.

He even carried the furled umbrella that last time I ever saw him in his dress-up clothes, so he must have thought too that it was an important occasion.

# EPILOGUE

A half century after I had planted my pin oak tree in a boyish gesture toward improving a bleak landscape, I went back to Grayson to see how it grew.

I went first to the Welcome Home Cemetery and saw for

the first time the twin marble markers on the graves of my grandparents. Carved in the stone were these words:

| FATHER | MOTHER |
|--------|--------|
| Marion C. | Margaret H. |
| Dec. 29, 1845 | Feb. 9, 1848 |
| April 15, 1925 | Sept. 12, 1924 |

BLACKMAN

Our Sacrificing Parents

There was nothing to indicate the identities of the children suggested by the word "Our" in the last chiseled line on the stone at the foot of the two graves. I felt a momentary pang of regret that my father could not have been among the contributors to the marble tribute.

The small frame building that was our First House was now painted white, but otherwise just as I remembered it, except—

It was a hot summer afternoon, but the once unshaded front porch now looked invitingly cool in the shadow of the stately pin oak tree, all of fifty spreading feet tall.

I thought how proud my grandfather surely would be if he could see it now. And I wondered wistfully if some of his pride might not be extended concomitantly to me, who had planted the sapling. But of that I could not be sure, for a man is not so easily measured as a tree.